A Bibliography of the Works of Katherine Anne Porter

and

A Bibliography of the Criticism of the Works of Katherine Anne Porter

by

Louise Waldrip

and

Shirley Ann Bauer

The Scarecrow Press, Inc.

Metuchen, N.J. 1969

Introduction

1969

Because of recent developments in Katherine Anne Porter's literary production and in critical attention given her, a complete and up-dated bibliography of the works and criticism seems in order. In 1962 Miss Porter's first full-length novel, Ship of Fools, remained on the best-seller list for forty-five weeks. In 1966 her The Collected Stories of Katherine Anne Porter received the seventeenth annual National Book Award for Fiction and the Pulitzer Prize for Fiction. Known mainly only to the literary-minded even three decades ago, Miss Porter's name is now familiar even to high school readers. Her work appears in most recent anthologies of best American writers. Revisers of older anthologies are also making a place for her in their later editions. Since 1962 two full-length books and two shorter monographs devoted entirely to a critical consideration of Miss Porter's works have appeared. This bibliography, which covers Miss Porter's entire career thus far, reflects the increasing critical appreciation of her writing.

The bibliography is divided into two main sections. The first was compiled by Louise Waldrip and the second by Shirley Ann Bauer. In the first section an attempt has been made to find all translations, introductions or afterwords to books, and all other types of contributions to books and periodicals written by Miss Porter up to and including some entries for 1968. The second section is a comprehensive listing of critical estimates of Miss Porter's works in books, periodicals and newspapers up to and including some entries for 1968. Miss Porter kindly made her collection of clippings available to the compiler so that the listings of newspaper reviews are more complete than they might otherwise have been. However, the listings in the bibliography do not represent Miss Porter's complete collection.

Like all bibliographies, this one is certain to be incomplete. Records of many of Miss Porter's early writings, especially those in

3

local newspapers, have been impossible to find. Exact dates of publication down to month and day, if not stated in the works themselves, have been filled in from Publishers' Weekly, Library of Congress catalog cards, Catalogue of the United States Copyright Office, British Museum Catalogue of Printed Books, English Catalogue of Books, Index Translationum, and letters from publishers. Measurements are given in inches. Bindings of books are described by the most commonly-used names of colors. Where page numbers are missing in Section B, "Contributions to Books," entries were taken from publishers' catalogs where only the name of the author and the title of the author's contribution were given.

It is known in bibliographical circles that publishers sometimes do not distinguish between a new printing of a book and a new edition. It is possible in a few cases, therefore, that the information on the verso of the title page may have led the compiler to label as a new edition an entry that was actually only a new printing.

The question may arise as to why a seventh edition, for example, of a particular anthology is listed in this bibliography when no earlier edition appears. Though this may not always be the answer, it has been found in some instances that earlier editions carried no work by Miss Porter. She was included only in the later revised editions.

Entries A1, A2, A3, A 10 and D2 were not available for examination. They are therefore described from photoduplicated copies of the covers and from some of the pages preliminary to the text, as well as from additional information furnished in letters from Library of Congress reference librarians.

In transcribing title pages of original work, differences in several sizes of type have been ignored. Thus words in capital letters on the title pages are typed in capitals, whether the originals are large capitals or small. Where two sizes of capital letters occur in the same line, the smaller ones are underlined twice. Words not in capitals are in ordinary typescript with only the first letter capitalized where it is capitalized on the title page. Words or complete lines in italics are so indicated by underlining. No attempt has been made at collating variations in editions with the Hinman Collator.

4

Works under "Original Contributions" which have Miss Porter's personal autograph or any other notation from her have been pointed out at the end of the entry. The bibliography of works is divided into four parts: A. Original Contributions, B. Contributions to Books, C. Contributions to Periodicals, D. Translations. Works in each part are arranged chronologically. In Section B, where more than one work occurs under the same date, they are arranged alphabetically by the title of the book. In Section C, multiple works under one year are arranged chronologically by months.

The bibliography of criticism is divided into five sections: E. Books and Sections of Books; F. Articles in Periodicals and Newspapers; G. Doctoral Dissertations and Masters' Theses; H. Foreign Language Material; and I. Book Reviews. Under E, F, G, and H, the listings are arranged alphabetically by author or by editor if no author is given. If no author or editor is given, the listings appear alphabetically by title, or, in the absence of a title, by the name of the publication. Under I, the listings are arranged alphabetically following the book with which the reviews are concerned. The books are arranged chronologically according to their publication dates with the exception of Flowering Judas and Other Stories. Although it was first published in 1930, most of the reviews are in response to the 1935 edition. Therefore, in order to give a chronological view of the critical response, it follows Hacienda, which appeared in 1934.

Other than the listings under "Foreign Language Material," all items have been verified except for those which are designated by a single asterisk. All items in Edward Schwartz' 1953 bibliography have been checked, with the exception of those listed with an asterisk. I did not list some of the articles in the New York Times which appear on p. 236 of Mr. Schwartz' bibliography because I was unable to find the articles mentioned in either the paper or the New York Times Index. Items not included are those dated June 20, 1942; September 29, 1944; May 19, 1948; and October 2, 1949. My annotations are taken from the articles described and not from Mr. Schwartz' descriptions. A double asterisk follows listings of clippings which were seen at Miss Porter's home but which I was unable to verify further for date or page number. No attempt was made to find all

5

foreign language listings, nor were the items listed verified except for H2 and H13, which were seen at Miss Porter's home. These entries are listed as they appear in various indexes. Under "Doctoral Dissertations and Masters' Theses," the two masters' theses were listed in George Hendricks' bibliography appended to his book, Katherine Anne Porter (E27). Numbers enclosed in parentheses following annotations are for the purpose of making cross references between related listings.

Under "Books and Sections of Books," titles of monographs have been typed in all-capital letters so that they may be distinguished from books that only have sections which deal with Miss Porter's writings. Articles concerning biographical material and announcements of awards made to Miss Porter are listed in the "Articles in Periodicals and Newspapers" section.

The compilers of this bibliography would like to express their gratitude to Miss Katherine Anne Porter for her encouragement and assistance. Mrs. Bauer is particularly indebted to Miss Porter, who graciously allowed her to see the collection of clippings in Miss Porter's home and who brought material to the compiler's attention. Mrs. Waldrip would like to thank Dr. Edwin T. Bowden and Dr. William B. Todd especially for their guidance in technical matters relating to bibliographical format. Mrs. Bauer would like to thank Dr. Jackson R. Bryer for his patience, advice and encouragement. Thanks are due the staffs of the McKeldin Library and the Library of Congress for much assistance received.

Table of Contents

A. ORIGINAL WORKS

1921   MY CHINESE MARRIAGE   A1

MY CHINESE / MARRIAGE / BY / M. T. F. / [ornament] /
NEW YORK / DUFFIELD AND COMPANY / 1921

(8-1/4 x 5-3/4): pp. viii, 170. (Copy examined has been rebound and
is so worn and torn out at the stitchings that it is impossible to count
the gatherings.)

Contents: [i-ii], half-title, verso blank; [iii-iv], title, on verso copyright notice; [v-vi], "To my Chinese father and mother with the
gratitude and affection of their American daughter this volume is
dedicated," verso blank; [vii-viii], table of contents, verso blank;
[1-170], text, verso of last leaf blank.

Copy examined was rebound in maroon cloth, spine titled in gilt.

In his bibliography Mr. Edward Schwartz states that Miss Porter had
written him that this book was "a mere setting down of someone else's
story, nothing of my own."

1922   OUTLINE OF MEXICAN POPULAR ARTS AND CRAFTS   A2

Outline of Mexican / Popular Arts and Crafts / By KATHERINE
ANNE PORTER / [double rule] / UPON the occasion of the /
Traveling Mexican Popular / Arts Exposition in the United / States
of North America, under / the auspices of the Ministry of /
Industry, Commerce and Labor / of Mexico, Don Xavier Guerrero,
/ being the Art Director, has / caused this book to be published.
/ It contains a study by Miss / Katherine Anne Porter, of the /
Popular Arts and Crafts of / Mexico. / Cover design by Xav.
Gro. / Photographs from the collection of / Roberto A. Turnbull /
[double rule] / Copyright, 1922, by S. I. C. y T.

(8-3/4 x 5-3/4): pp. 56.

Contents: [1-2], title, on verso, acknowledgement; [3], fly-title
above a large reproduction of a decorated jar by Tonalá, Jalisco;
4-56, text.

Issued in off-white paper cover displaying replicas in brown of seven
woodcuts of Mexican art arranged in a square, underneath which is
title of book and name of author in brown letters; at lower right in
black type:

A Souvenir of the "MEXICAN NIGHT" held at the
National Museum under the auspices of the "PAN
AMERICAN STUDENTS' ASSOCIATION of the
SCHOOL OF FOREIGN SERVICE, GEORGETOWN
UNIVERSITY, Washington, April 5, 1923. [Quotation
beginning at "Pan American" is not closed with quota-
tion marks in the copy described.]

1927   WHAT PRICE MARRIAGE   A3

What Price / Marriage / with / INTRODUCTION AND NOTES /
[ornament] / [quotation beneath ornament:] "With the wind of God
in her / vesture, proclaiming the deathless, / eversoaring spirit
of man."--Locke / J. H. SEARS & COMPANY, Inc. / PUB-
LISHERS / NEW YORK

(6-3/4 x 4-1/4): pp. 262.

Contents: [1-2], title, on verso, copyright notice and other publisher's material; [3-4], "Foreword to The Royal Collection" (signed:
The Publishers), verso blank; 5-6, table of contents; 7-14, introduction, verso of last leaf blank.

Issued case-bound in red leather-grained cloth, gilt medallion on
front cover and gilt lettering on spine; gold-colored end papers in
faint heraldic design.

CONTENTS

1930   FLOWERING JUDAS   A4

KATHERINE ANNE PORTER / [narrow rule] / FLOWERING / JUDAS / [ornament] / [narrow rule] / HARCOURT, BRACE AND COMPANY / New York

(8-1/3 x 5-3/8): $[1-10]^8$ (10_8 is pasted-down end paper), pp. x, 150.

Contents: [i-ii], half-title, verso blank; [iii-iv], title, on verso copyright notice, "First edition, limited to 600 copies," and other publisher's matter, including imprint; [v-vi], "For Susan Jenkins," verso blank; [vii-viii], acknowledgements, verso blank; [ix-x], table of contents, verso blank; [1-2], fly-title, verso blank; 3-[146], text, verso of last leaf blank; [147-150], blank. Yellow publisher's slip accompanying book states: "Edition limited to 600 copies."

Issued in beige boards with brown cloth half-binding. Boards show heavy watermark. Top edges of pages stained pale yellow; white end papers.

The first edition was published 11 September 1930.

CONTENTS

"Maria Concepción"

First appeared in Century Magazine, December 1922.

"Magic"

First appeared in transition, Summer 1928.

"Rope"

> First appeared in The Second American Caravan, ed. A.
> Kreymborg. New York: The Macaulay Company, 1928.

"He"

> First appeared in New Masses, October 1927.

"The Jilting of Granny Weatherall"

> First appeared in transition, February 1929.

"Flowering Judas"

> First appeared in Hound and Horn, Spring 1930.

The University of Texas copy No. 60-372 in Rare Books Collection
is inscribed by the author: "For the Southern Literature Collection
with good wishes. Katherine Anne Porter, Austin, 22 October
1958."

1934   HACIENDA   A5

[ornament] / HACIENDA / KATHERINE ANNE PORTER /
HARRISON OF PARIS

$(8-3/4 \times 6)$: $[1-9]^4 [10]^6$, pp. 84.

Contents: [1-2], "Hacienda, This the thirteenth publication of Harrison of Paris, has been designed by Monroe Wheeler and printed in
twelve-point linotype Baskerville italic by The Haddon Craftsmen at
Camden, New Jersey, in November, 1934. [New paragraph begins
here, but there is no space between paragraphs.] The edition consists of eight hundred and ninety-five copies of Arnold English un-
bleached pure-rag paper, 1-895, of which this is number 28" [28
is written in by hand], verso blank; [3-4], title, on verso copyright
notice; [5-6], "Hacienda, All characters and situations in this story
are entirely fictional, and do not portray any actual person," verso
blank; [7-82], text, verso of last leaf blank; [83-84], blank.

Issued in maroon cloth; spine titled in gilt; top edges of pages gilt.
Slip-in case of chartreuse; on front, enclosed in maroon box, title
and publisher's blurb in gilt with statement: "Edition limited to
895 copies."

The first edition was published 7 December 1934.

The British Museum General Catalogue of Printed Books lists this
novel as published by Harrison of Paris in New York in 1934, no

month given, but the English Catalogue of Books gives the date as
January 1935. The United States Copyright Office Catalogue lists it
as copyrighted 7 December 1934.
The University of Texas copy No. 60-375 in the Rare Books Collection is inscribed by the author: "For the Southern Literature Collection with good wishes from Katherine Anne Porter, Austin, 22
October 1958."

1935   FLOWERING JUDAS AND OTHER STORIES   A6
a. Flowering Judas / AND OTHER STORIES / BY KATHERINE
ANNE PORTER / [ornament] / HARCOURT, BRACE AND COM-
PANY / NEW YORK
$(8 \times 5\text{-}3/8)$: $[1\text{-}18]^8$ $[19]^4$, pp. vi, 290.
Contents: [i-ii], half-title, on verso: "This collection contains all
of the stories which appeared in the original limited edition of
Flowering Judas and Other Stories, together with four new stories,
'Theft,' 'That Tree,' 'The Cracked Looking-Glass,' and 'Hacienda'";
[iii-iv], title, on verso copyright notice, imprint, and other publisher's matter; [v-vi], table of contents, verso blank; [1-286], text,
verso of last leaf blank; [287-290], blank. [Quotation on verso of
half-title page is in error. The original limited edition was entitled merely Flowering Judas.]
Issued in pale beige cloth titled in green; spine titled downward in
green; white end papers; top edges of pages stained pale brown.
Dust jacket; author's name and publisher's announcement of new
stories added to this edition in green on beige background shaded in
vertical strips, title in white beneath two green horizontal dividing
bars; spine titled in white on beige with green vertical bar; on back,
advertisement of Virginia Woolf's work; on inside front flap, publisher's blurb; on inside back flap, biographical note.
The first edition was published 12 October 1935.
A variant issue gives the copyright by Harcourt, Brace and Company [1935] instead of by Katherine Anne Porter as does the issue
described. An ornament and some of the publisher's matter are
omitted on the copyright page of this variant. Colors of binding
and dust jacket are slightly darker, but top edges of pages are

stained a lighter brown.

CONTENTS

"Maria Concepción"

First appeared in Century Magazine, December 1922.

"Magic"

First appeared in transition, Summer 1928.

"Rope"

First appeared in The Second American Caravan, ed. A.
Kreymborg. New York: The Macaulay Co., 1928.

"He"

First appeared in New Masses, October 1927.

"Theft"

First appeared in The Gyroscope, November 1929.

"That Tree"

First appeared in Virginia Quarterly Review, July 1934.

"The Jilting of Granny Weatherall"

First appeared in transition, February 1929.

"Flowering Judas"

First appeared in Hound and Horn, Spring 1930.

"The Cracked Looking-Glass"

First appeared in Scribner's Magazine, May 1932.

"Hacienda"

First appeared in Virginia Quarterly Review, October 1932.
The University of Texas copy No. 60-373 in the Rare Books Collection is inscribed: "For the Southern Literature Collection, on the
day I was in Austin, 22nd October 1958, with good wishes. Katherine Anne Porter. 'It doth make a difference whence cometh a man's
joy.' St. Augustine."

b. First English edition:

London: Jonathan Cape. (7-3/4 x 5): pp. 288. Published April
1936. (Not seen. From English Catalogue of Books.)

1937   NOON WINE   A7

a. NOON / WINE / by / KATHERINE / ANNE / POR-
TER / [ornament] / SCHUMAN'S 1937 DETROIT

(10 x 6-3/8): [1]^4 [2-5]^8 [6]^4 (first and last leaves are pasted

down for end papers), pp. vi, 65. In gatherings [2-5] leaves 5-6,
7-8 are unopened on outer edge.

Contents: [i-iv], blank; [v-vi], half-title above ornamental rule,
"Time: 1896-1905, Place: Small South Texas farm," verso blank;
[1-2], title, on verso copyright notice; [3-4], fly-title, verso blank;
[5]-65, text; [66], certificate limiting issue to 250 copies and
statement: "This edition, printed by Peter Beilenson at the Walpole
Printing Office, Mount Vernon, New York, consists of two hundred
fifty copies for sale."

Issued in decorated binding of fabricated material, title on buff paper label enclosed in black and green border. Slip-in case of
greenish gray.

First edition published 20 February 1937. This story was previously published in Signatures, Spring 1936. It later appeared in Story,
June 1937.

Copies Nos. 66 and 136 in the Rare Books Collection at The University of Texas are signed by the author.

b. LE VIN DE MIDI. Paris, Editions du Pavois, 1948. 16°, pp.
304. A translation, by Marcelle Sibon. (Not seen. From Index
Translationum.)

1939   PALE HORSE, PALE RIDER   A8

a. KATHERINE ANNE PORTER / PALE HORSE, / PALE
RIDER / Three Short Novels / [publisher's emblem:] hb /
HARCOURT, BRACE AND COMPANY, NEW YORK
(8 x 5-3/8): [1-17]^{8}, pp. viii, 264.

Contents: [i-ii], half-title, on verso notice of an earlier book by
the same author; [iii-iv], title, on verso copyright notice and imprint; [v-vi], "To Harrison Boone Porter," verso blank; [vii-viii],
table of contents, verso blank; [1]-264, text.

Issued in blue-gray cloth, front and spine titled in black; top edges
of pages stained yellow; white end papers.

Dust jacket: title in black letters shaded in teal blue against white
oval on teal blue background, list of contents in white and teal blue
set in a black box, author's name and title of an earlier book in
white set in a smaller black box; spine titled in black against white

oval on very pale teal blue background imprinted with: "Three Short Novels by Katherine Anne Porter" and publisher's name in teal blue and white in black box; on back, advertisement for Flowering Judas and Other Stories; on inside front flap, publisher's blurb; on inside back flap, biographical note on author.

The first edition was published 1 April 1939.

CONTENTS

"Old Mortality"

First appeared in The Southern Review, Spring 1938.

"Noon Wine"

First appeared in Signatures, Spring 1936.

"Pale Horse, Pale Rider"

First appeared in The Southern Review, Winter 1938.

A second impression was issued in April 1939 and a third in May 1939. A variant impression of uncertain date omits any reference to either edition or impression on the copyright page and also omits the name of the printer. Top edges of this copy are not stained, and gatherings are $[1\text{-}7]^{16}$ $[8]^8$ $[9]^{16}$. Color of binding is pale green.

The copy in the Barker History Collection of The University of Texas is signed on half-title page: "Best Regards Katherine Anne Porter."

b. First English edition:

London: Jonathan Cape. Published May 1939; printed in the United States. (Not seen. From British Museum General Catalogue of Printed Books.)

c. Ai To Shi No Kage Ni.--Masao Takahashi.--Tokyo, Dabiddo-sha. 177. [n.d.] (Japanese translation of Pale Horse, Pale Rider).

d. Susunan Lama [Diterdjemahkan oleh Mochtar Lubis]. Djakarta, Balai Pustaka, 1950. (Indonesian translation of Pale Horse, Pale Rider).

1944   THE LEANING TOWER AND OTHER STORIES   A9

a. KATHERINE ANNE PORTER / THE / LEANING TOWER / AND OTHER STORIES / [publisher's emblem:] hb / HARCOURT, BRACE AND COMPANY, NEW YORK

$(8 \times 5\text{-}1/4)$: $[1\text{-}8]^{16}$, pp. viii, 248.

Contents: [i-ii], half-title, on verso list of author's other works; [iii-iv], title, on verso copyright notice and other publisher's matter; [v-vi], "To Corporal Harrison Paul Porter, Jr.," verso blank; [vii-viii], table of contents, verso blank; [1]-246, text; [247-248], blank.

Identification of edition on copyright page: First edition.

Issued in putty-colored cloth titled in olive green; spine titled in olive green; top edges of pages stained olive green.

Dust jacket: on front, solid green background with title in black against stippled green box surrounded by decorative square border in white, author's name in white against gun-metal gray box outlined in black and white frame lines; on back and continuing on inside back flap, excerpts from newspaper and magazine reviews of book; publisher's blurb on inside front flap.

The first edition was published 16 September 1944.

Subsequent impressions may be identified on copyright page as follows:

2.	b·9·44	6.	F·3·53
3.	c·10·44	7.	G·I·59
4.	d·10·44	8.	H·6·62
5.	e·I·48	9.	I·4·66

Another impression gives no code number or any other identification on the copyright page. All of the publisher's matter is omitted except "Published in the United States of America."

CONTENTS

"The Source"

    First appeared in <u>Accent</u>, Spring 1941.

"The Witness"

    First appeared here.

"The Circus"

    First appeared in <u>The Southern Review</u>, July 1935.

"The Old Order"

    First appeared in <u>The Southern Review</u>, Winter 1936.

"The Last Leaf"

    First appeared here.

"The Grave"

First appeared in Virginia Quarterly Review, April 1935.

"The Downward Path to Wisdom"

First appeared in Harper's Bazaar, December 1939.

"A Day's Work"

First appeared in Nation, 10 February 1940.

"The Leaning Tower"

First appeared in The Southern Review, Autumn 1941.

The University of Texas copy No. 60-376 in the Rare Books Collection is inscribed by the author on recto of free front end-paper: "Katherine Anne Porter 17 March 1937"; on half-title recto: "The signature on the fly-leaf is one of those I do for bookshops. When asked to sign books in stock-- When I sign for a friend or institution or Book Collection, I always write the name and date, So-- For the Southern Literature Collection, University of Texas, with good wishes, October 22, 1955, Katherine Anne Porter."
A second University of Texas copy, No. 4-27 in the Rare Books Collection, is inscribed by the author: "Katherine Anne Porter 22 October 1958."

b. First English edition (1945):

THE / LEANING / TOWER / and Other Stories / by /
KATHERINE ANNE PORTER / [ornament] / JONATHAN CAPE
/ THIRTY BEDFORD SQUARE / LONDON
(7-1/2 x 4-7/8): [A]-L^8, pp. 176.

Contents: [1-2], half-title, on verso list of other books by the same author; [3-4], title, on verso: "First published 1945, " publisher's imprint, ornament, and other publisher's matter; 5-6, table of contents, on verso: "To Corporal Harrison Paul Porter, Jr. ";
7-[174], text, verso of last leaf blank; [175-176], blank.
Identification of edition on copyright page: First published 1945.
Issued in beige cloth titled in green; spine titled in green; top edges of pages unstained.
Contents identical with A9a, but a comparison of the two books shows that the original plates were not used.
The first English edition was published in October 1945.

c. First Danish edition (1948):

Porter, Katherine Anne, DET SKAEVE TAARN.--Ole Jacobsen.--
København, Det danske Forlag, 1948, 8⁰. 256. Kr. 6,50. (Not
seen. From Index Translationum.)

d. First German edition (1953):

Porter, Katherine Anne. Das Letzte Blatt.--Hans Bochow--
Blüthgen.--Bad Wörishofen, Kindler & Schiermeyer, 1953. 247,
7.85.

e. First French edition (1954):

Porter, (Katherine-Anne).--La Tour Penchée. Trad. par Marcelle
Sibon. (14/19, 208 p. Br.: 450 fr. (1954). Edit. du Seuil.

1945   SELECTED SHORT STORIES   A10
[The cover of this book is the real title-page and is thus trans-
cribed:]
SELECTED SHORT STORIES OF / KATHERINE / ANNE /
PORTER / Overseas edition for the Armed Forces. Distrib- /
uted by the Special Services Division, A.S.F., / for the Army,
and by the Bureau of Naval / Personnel for the Navy. U. S.
Government prop- / erty. Not for sale. Published by Editions
for the / Armed Services, Inc., a non-profit organization /
established by the Council on Books in Wartime. /
[At upper left, the series number R-21. At left, reproduction of
an imaginary conventional hardcover edition and "ARMED SERVICES
EDITION" in circle. At foot, "SELECTED SHORT STORIES." In
red, yellow, green, black, and white.]
(3-13/16 x 5-7/16): Stapled paperback edition. In copy examined,
gatherings not definable.)
Contents: [1-2], "PUBLISHED BY ARRANGEMENT WITH HAR-
COURT, BRACE AND COMPANY, INC., NEW YORK / Selected
Stories / of / KATHERINE ANNE PORTER / Editions for
the Armed Services, Inc. / A NON-PROFIT ORGANIZATION ES-
TABLISHED BY THE COUNCIL ON BOOKS IN WARTIME, NEW
YORK"; on verso copyright notice and other publisher's matter; [3-
4], table of contents, verso blank; 5-[320], text, verso of last leaf
contains only a small device.
Issued in paper covers with front cover as title-cover described

above; spine titled downward with series number R-21 on lower edge; on back, "SELECTED SHORT STORIES of Katherine Anne Porter," under which are three paragraphs commenting on Miss Porter's work followed by: "This special edition of SELECTED SHORT STORIES of Katherine Anne Porter has / been made available to the Armed Forces of the United States through an arrange- / ment with the original publisher, Harcourt, Brace and Company, New York. / Editions for the Armed Services, Inc., a non-profit organization established by the Council on Books in Wartime." The entire back cover is surrounded by an ornamental border. On inside front cover is a statement of nine lines entitled "ARMED SERVICES EDITION." (Mr. Trienens states that it does not relate specifically to the book described.) On inside back cover are listed editions R-1 through R-40 under the heading "OTHER ARMED SERVICES EDITIONS INCLUDE:"

Mr. Roger J. Trienens, Reference Librarian at The Library of Congress to whom I am indebted for most of the above information, writes: "A Library of Congress stamp on the verso of the title page indicates that the volume was received as a gift of the publisher on 4 June 1945."

CONTENTS

"Maria Concepción"

    First appeared in Century Magazine, December 1922.

"That Tree"

    First appeared in Virginia Quarterly Review, July 1934.

"The Grave"

    First appeared in Virginia Quarterly Review, April 1935.

"The Cracked Looking-Glass"

    First appeared in Scribner's Magazine, May 1932.

"The Downward Path to Wisdom"

    First appeared in Harper's Bazaar, December 1939.

"The Witness"

    First appeared in The Leaning Tower and Other Stories.

    New York: Harcourt, Brace and Company, 1944

"The Old Order"

    First appeared in The Southern Review, Winter 1936.

"Hacienda"

First appeared in Virginia Quarterly Review, October 1932.

"Noon Wine"

First appeared in Signatures, Spring 1936.

1952   THE DAYS BEFORE   A11

a. The Days Before / BY KATHERINE ANNE PORTER / [ornament] / Harcourt, Brace and Company / New York

(8 x 5-1/4): [1-9]^{16}, pp. x, 276.

Contents: blank leaf; [i-ii], half-title, on verso list of other books by the same author; [iii-iv], title, on verso copyright notice; [v-vi], "FOR GAY PORTER HOLLAWAY, " verso blank; vii-viii, foreword; ix-x, table of contents; [1-276], text, verso of last leaf blank; [275-276], blank.

Issued in pale teal blue cloth titled in dark blue; spine titled downward in dark blue; white end papers.

Dust jacket contains replica of pencil drawing of author on white background, title in red, author's name in black; spine titled downward in red, author's and publisher's names in black; on back, excerpts from reviews of other works by author; on inside front and back flaps, publisher's blurb and biographical note.

The first edition was published 25 October 1952.

CONTENTS

Critical

"The Days Before"

First appeared in Kenyon Review, Autumn 1943.

"On a Criticism of Thomas Hardy"

First appeared in The Southern Review, Summer 1940.

"Gertrude Stein: Three Views"

"Everybody Is a Real One"--first appeared in New York Herald Tribune Books, 16 January 1927, as a review of The Making of Americans by Gertrude Stein.

"Second Wind"--first appeared in New York Herald Tribune Books, 23 September 1928, as a parody of a review of Gertrude Stein's Useful Knowledge.

"The Wooden Umbrella"--first appeared in Harper's Maga-

zine, December 1947, under the title of "Gertrude Stein: a
Self-Portrait. "

"Reflections on Willa Cather"

First appeared in Mademoiselle, July 1952.

"It Is Hard to Stand in the Middle"

First appeared as "Yours, Ezra Pound" in the New York
Times Book Review, 29 October 1950. A review of The
Letters of Ezra Pound, 1907-1941, edited by D.D. Paige.

"The Art of Katherine Mansfield"

First appeared in the Nation, 23 October 1937.

"Orpheus in Purgatory"

First appeared in the New York Times Book Review, 1 January 1950.

"The Laughing Heat of the Sun"

First appeared as "Edith Sitwell's Steady Growth" in the
New York Herald Tribune Book Review, 18 December 1949.
A review of The Canticle of the Rose, 1917-1949, by Edith
Sitwell.

"Eudora Welty and 'A Curtain of Green'"

First appeared in the introduction to Eudora Welty's A Curtain of Green and Other Stories. New York: Doubleday,
Doran and Company, Inc., 1941.

"Homage to Ford Madox Ford"

First appeared in New Directions, Number 7, ed. James
Laughlin. Norfolk, Connecticut: New Directions, 1942.

"Virginia Woolf"

First appeared as "Virginia Woolf's Essays--a Great Art, a
Sober Craft" in the New York Times Book Review, 7 May
1950. Review of The Captain's Death Bed and Other Essays
by Virginia Woolf.

"E.M. Forster"

First appeared as "E.M. Forster Speaks Out for the Things
He Holds Dear" in the New York Times Book Review, 4
November 1951. Review of Two Cheers for Democracy by
E.M. Forster.

Personal and Particular

"Three Statements About Writing"

"1931: The Situation in American Writing"

First appeared as "Symposium: The Situation in American Writing, " in Partisan Review, Summer 1939.

"1940: Introduction to 'Flowering Judas'"

First appeared as the introduction to the first Modern
Library edition of Flowering Judas and Other Stories,
1940.

"1942: Transplanted Writers"

First appeared in Books Abroad, July 1942.

"No Plot, My Dear, No Story"

First appeared in Writer, June 1942.

"The Flower of Flowers"; with a note on "Pierre-Joseph Redouté"

First appeared in Flair, May 1950.

"Portrait: Old South"

First appeared in Mademoiselle, February 1944; reprinted in
Scholastic, 3 April 1944.

"Audubon's Happy Land"

First appeared as "Happy Land" in Vogue, 1 November 1939.

"A House of My Own"

First appeared as "Now at Last a House of My Own" in
Vogue, 1 September 1941.

"The Necessary Enemy"

First appeared as "Love and Hate" in Mademoiselle, October
1948.

"Marriage Is Belonging"

First appeared in Mademoiselle, October 1951.

"American Statement: 4 July 1942"

First appeared in Mademoiselle, July 1942.

"The Future Is Now"

First appeared in Mademoiselle, November 1950.

Mexican

"Notes on the Life and Death of a Hero"

First appeared as the preface to The Itching Parrot (El

Periquillo Sarniento) by José Joaquín Fernández de Lizárdi.
Translated from the Spanish by Katherine Anne Porter.
Garden City, New York: Doubleday, Doran and Co., Inc.,
1942.

"Why I Write About Mexico"
First appeared as a letter to the editor of The Century, 1923.

"Leaving the Petate"
First appeared in New Republic, 4 February 1931.

"The Mexican Trinity"
First appeared in The Freeman, 3 August 1921.

"La Conquistadora"
First appeared in New York Herald Tribune Books, 11 April
1926. Review of The Rosalie Evans Letters from Mexico
edited by D.D. Pettus.

"Quetzalcoatl"
First appeared in New York Herald Tribune Books, 7 March
1926. Review of The Plumed Serpent by D.H. Lawrence.

"The Charmed Life"
First appeared in Vogue, 15 April 1942.

b. First English edition:
London: Secker & Warburg, 1953. Pp. 273. (Not seen. From
British Museum General Catalogue of Printed Books.)

1955   A DEFENSE OF CIRCE   A12
Katherine Anne Porter / A DEFENSE OF CIRCE / * / Harcourt, Brace and Company . New York
(7-1/2 x 4-5/8): [1-3]^4, pp. 24.

Contents: [1-2], half-title, verso blank; [3-4], "MCMLV This first
edition is limited to 1700 copies privately printed for the friends of
the author and her publishers as a New Year's greeting," verso
blank; [5-6], title, on verso copyright notice and other publisher's
matter; [7-8], fly-title, verso blank; [9-22], text; [23-24], blank.
Issued in boards covered with paper marbled in shades of blue with
touches of rust and gold; white paper label printed with title and
name of author in blue and black on front cover.
The first edition was published 8 January 1955. First appeared in

Mademoiselle (June 1954).

1955   THE OLD ORDER   A13

Katherine Anne Porter / THE OLD ORDER / STORIES OF
THE SOUTH / FROM Flowering Judas, / Pale Horse, Pale
Rider AND / The Leaning Tower / A HARVEST BOOK /
Harcourt, Brace & World, Inc. / New York
(7-1/4 x 4-1/4): pp. vi, 186. [This book is a "Harvest Book"
paperback, but it is described in full because there seems to have
been no previous hardback issue.]

Contents: [i-ii], half-title, on verso brief literary biography; [iii-iv],
title, on verso copyright notice, "G. 8. 62, " and other publisher's matter;
[v-vi], table of contents, verso blank; [1-2], fly-title, verso blank; 3-
182, text; [183-186], blank.

Issued in rose-colored paper cover; large black rose on front with author's name in black across the middle of the cover, title beneath author's name, broad buff-colored band across bottom edge imprinted in
white with: "Stories of the South from her books THE LEANING TOW-
ER, PALE HORSE, PALE RIDER, FLOWERING JUDAS"; imprinted on
lower edge in black: "HB6, " "HARVEST BOOKS, " and price of book;
spine titled downward in white with author's name in black, "HARVEST
HB6" in black at lower edge; on back, against rose and buff background,
"A HARVEST BOOK" and author's name in black, title in white, publisher's note on source and nature of stories and "COVER DESIGN BY SUS-
AN FOSTER" in black, and name of publisher in white.

The first edition was published 6 August 1955. Concerning this edition, Publisher's Weekly for this date states: "The first time all
the author's southern [sic] stories have been brought together in one
volume. "
                            CONTENTS
"The Old Order"
        "The Source"
                First appeared in Accent, Spring 1941.
        "The Old Order"
                First appeared in The Southern Review, Winter 1936.
        "The Witness"

First appeared in The Leaning Tower and Other Stories
by Katherine Anne Porter. New York: Harcourt,
Brace and Company, 1944.

"The Circus"

First appeared in The Southern Review, July 1935.

"The Last Leaf"

First appeared in The Leaning Tower and Other Stories
by Katherine Anne Porter. New York: Harcourt,
Brace and Company, 1944.

"The Grave"

First appeared in Virginia Quarterly Review, April
1935.

"The Jilting of Granny Weatherall"

First appeared in transition, February 1929.

"He"

First appeared in New Masses, October 1927.

"Magic"

First appeared in transition, Summer 1928.

"Old Mortality"

First appeared in The Southern Review, Spring 1938.

Two other impressions in "Harvest Books" paperbacks are identified
by "H.1.63" imprinted on the copyright page of one and "1.9.64" on
the copyright page of the other. These numbers would seem to indicate that the book has gone through at least nine printings.

1958   A CHRISTMAS STORY   A14

KATHERINE ANNE PORTER / [French rule] / A / CHRIST-
MAS / STORY / [French rule] / MADEMOISELLE / 1958
(4 x 9-7/8): [1-2]^{16}, pp. viii, 24.

Contents: [i-ii], blank; [iii-iv], title, on verso imprint and copyright notice; [v-vi], drawing of open rose with one bud and two
leaves with "THIS IS OUR CHRISTMAS CARD TO YOU" imprinted
beneath, verso blank; [vii-viii], author's name imprinted, verso
blank; 1-20, text; [21-22], blank; [23-24], duplicate of the rose design on page [v] and statement "Designed by Tammis Keefe," verso
blank.

Issued in white boards, rose design in rose color on front cover
with title, name of author, and name of publisher imprinted in
black; identical rose design placed upside down on back cover with
"CHRISTMAS 1958" imprinted beneath; spine titled in black; rose-
colored end papers sprinkled with small rosebud silhouettes in a
brownish-rose color.

This story first appeared in Mademoiselle, December 1946, and
was later reprinted in Scholastic, December 1947. The issue described here is a simulated Christmas card, which, according to a
staff member of Mademoiselle, consisted of perhaps 2500 to 3000
copies. These were given only to Mademoiselle staff members as
a Christmas gift in 1958, and no copies were sold to the public.

1960   RECENT SOUTHERN FICTION: A15
                A PANEL DISCUSSION

Recent Southern Fiction: / A Panel Discussion / KATHERINE
/ ANNE PORTER / FLANNERY O'CONNOR / CAROLINE
GORDON / MADISON JONES / LOUIS D. RUBIN, JR., MOD-
ERATOR / OCTOBER 28, 1960 / WESLEYAN COLLEGE /
MACON, GEORGIA

(9-3/4 x 6-3/4): [1]^8, pp. 16.

Contents: [1]-2, foreword, on verso list of participants in panel
with a brief paragraph identifying each; 3-16, text.

Issued in buff-colored marble board with title [as above] on front
cover; on back, imprinted between two sets of double horizontal
rules: "BULLETIN OF WESLEYAN COLLEGE, VOLUME 41, JAN-
UARY, 1961, NUMBER 1, Published quarterly in January, April,
July, and October by Wesleyan College, Macon, Georgia. Entered
as second-class matter June 1, 1923 at the Post Office at Macon,
Georgia, under the Act of August 24, 1912, at the special rate of
postage provided for in section 1103, Act of October 3, 1917."
First published January 1961.

1962   SHIP OF FOOLS   A16
a. Katherine Anne Porter / SHIP OF FOOLS / [ornament] /
An Atlantic Monthly Press Book / Little, Brown and Company ·

Boston · Toronto

$(8-1/4 \times 5-5/8)$: $[1-16]^{16}$, pp. xiv, 498.

Contents: [i-ii], half-title, on verso notice of author's previous books; [iii-iv], title, on verso copyright notice, "FIRST EDITION," and other publisher's matter; [v-vi], "For Barbara Wescott 1932: Paris, Rambouillet, Davosplatz, Salzburg, Munich, New York, Mulhocaway, Rosemont :1962," verso blank; [vii-viii], author's explanation of origin and general meaning of allegory of book, verso blank; [ix-x], table of contents, verso blank; xi-xiv, list of characters, verso of last leaf blank; [1-498], text, verso of last leaf blank.

Identification of edition on copyright page: FIRST EDITION.

Issued in yellow cloth boards with author's signature in dark red; spine titled in dark red with ornament and publisher's name in dark red; end papers marbled in shades of plum and black flecked with yellow.

Dust jacket: on front, author's name in yellow, title in white on marbled background of plum and black flecked with yellow; spine black titled in yellow with names of author and publisher in white; on back, photograph of author at desk.

The first edition was published 16 April 1962.

The September 1963 Signet Edition states that the hardcover edition has gone through eight printings and that the novel has been on the best-seller lists for forty-five weeks.

b. First English edition:

KATHERINE ANNE PORTER / SHIP OF FOOLS / [double bar] / LONDON / Secker & Warburg

$(8 \times 5-1/2)$: $[A]-Q^{16}$, pp. 512.

Contents: [1-2], introduction, on verso list of other books by author; [3-4], title, on verso copyright notice and imprint with other publisher's matter; [5-6], "FOR BARBARA WESTCOTT / 1932: Paris, Rambouillet, Davosplatz, Salzburg, Munich, New York, Mulhocaway, Rosemont :1962," on verso note by author explaining significance of title; 7-8, table of contents, on verso list of characters with their identification; 9-10, list of characters continued; [11-512], text.

Issued in gray paper boards titled in black.

Dust jacket: on front and spine, title in black, author's name in white between two black bars on blue-green background, woodcut type picture of ship loaded with court jesters in black; on back, photograph of author accompanied by biographical statement.

The first English edition was published October 1962.

1964   COLLECTED STORIES   A17

a. KATHERINE ANNE PORTER / COLLECTED STORIES [Title and name of author extend across two pages.] / [ornament] / BY THE SAME AUTHOR / SHIP OF FOOLS / JONATHAN CAPE / 30 BEDFORD SQUARE LONDON

(7-3/8 x 5): [A]-N^{16} O^{20} P^{16}, pp. 488.

Contents: [1], half-title and note by publisher; [2-3], title; [4], dates of earlier publication of stories in this collection, copyright notice, and imprint; [5-6], table of contents, verso blank; 7-[488], text, verso of last leaf blank.

Issued in dark mauve cloth, spine titled in gilt with gilt ornament; top edges of pages stained violet.

Dust jacket: ornamental gunmetal and white background with wide black band titled in white with author's name in violet; spine titled in white with author's name and ornament in violet on black band against ornamental gunmetal background; back solid violet; on inside front flap, excerpts from reviews of this book; on inside back flap, short biographical sketch of author.

The first edition was published 9 January 1964.

CONTENTS

"Go Little Book . . ."

Flowering Judas and Other Stories

"Maria Concepción"

First appeared in Century Magazine, December 1922.

"Virgin Violeta"

First appeared in Century Magazine, December 1924.

"The Martyr"

First appeared in Century Magazine, July 1923.

"Magic"

       First appeared in <u>transition</u>, Summer 1928.

"Rope"

       First appeared in <u>The Second American Caravan</u>, ed. A.

       Kreymborg. New York: The Macaulay Co., 1928.

"He"

       First appeared in <u>New Masses</u>, October 1927.

"Theft"

       First appeared in <u>The Gyroscope</u>, November 1929.

"That Tree"

       First appeared in <u>Virginia Quarterly Review</u>, July 1934.

"The Jilting of Granny Weatherall"

       First appeared in <u>transition</u>, February 1929.

"Flowering Judas"

       First appeared in <u>Hound and Horn</u>, Spring 1930.

"The Cracked Looking-Glass"

       First appeared in <u>Scribner's Magazine</u>, May 1932.

"Hacienda"

       First appeared in <u>Virginia Quarterly Review</u>, October 1932.

<u>Pale Horse, Pale Rider</u>

"Old Mortality"

       First appeared in <u>The Southern Review</u>, Spring 1938.

"Noon Wine"

       First appeared in <u>Signatures</u>, Spring 1936.

"Pale Horse, Pale Rider"

       First appeared in <u>The Southern Review</u>, Winter 1938.

<u>The Leaning Tower and Other Stories</u>

"The Old Order"

       First appeared in <u>The Southern Review</u>, Winter 1936.

"The Source"

       First appeared in <u>Accent</u>, Spring 1941.

"The Journey"

       First appeared in <u>The Southern Review</u>, Winter 1936, as

       part of "The Old Order."

"The Witness"

First appeared in <u>The Leaning Tower and Other Stories</u> by Katherine Anne Porter. New York: Harcourt, Brace and Company, 1944.

"The Circus"

First appeared in <u>The Southern Review</u>, July 1935.

"The Last Leaf"

First appeared in <u>The Leaning Tower and Other Stories</u> by Katherine Anne Porter. New York: Harcourt, Brace and Company, 1944.

"The Fig Tree"

First appeared in <u>Harper's Magazine</u>, June 1960.

"The Grave"

First appeared in <u>Virginia Quarterly Review</u>, April 1935.

"The Downward Path to Wisdom"

First appeared in <u>Harper's Bazaar</u>, December 1939.

"A Day's Work"

First appeared in <u>Nation</u>, 10 February 1940.

"Holiday"

First appeared in <u>Atlantic Monthly</u>, December 1960.

"The Leaning Tower"

First appeared in <u>The Southern Review</u>, Autumn 1941.

b. First American edition (1965):

The Collected Stories of / Katherine Anne Porter / Harcourt, Brace & World, Inc. [ornament]

(8-1/4 x 5-5/8): [1-16]^{16}, pp. 1 blank leaf, viii, 502 (last gathering has last leaf missing).

Contents: blank leaf; [i-ii], half-title, on verso list of other books by same author; [iii-iv], title, on verso copyright notice and "First American edition 1965"; [v-vi], introduction entitled "Go, Little Book . . ."; [vii-viii], table of contents: [1-496], text, verso of last leaf blank; [497-502], blank.

Identification of edition on copyright page: FIRST AMERICAN EDITION 1965.

Issued in blue cloth boards, spine titled in gilt; orange end papers; top edges of pages stained dark blue.

The first American edition was published 27 September 1965.

Contents and first appearance are identical with A17a.

A later impression is identified by "B.10.65" on copyright page.

A variant in gatherings was noted in this edition. The first leaf in the first gathering was missing, leaving that gathering with only fifteen leaves instead of the sixteen in all the other gatherings, and the shade of blue with which the top edges of the pages were stained was not identical with the shade on the book described.

c. Book-of-the-Month Club edition: Identical with the B.10.65 impression of A17b. Identified by a small impression in blind at lower right-hand corner of back cover.

B. CONTRIBUTIONS TO BOOKS

1928

THE SECOND AMERICAN CARAVAN, ed. A. Kreymborg.   B1
New York: The Macaulay Company, 1928.
Miss Porter contributed:
"Rope." Pp. 362-368.
    First appeared here. Reprinted in Scholastic, Vol.
XXVIII, 7 March 1936.

1930

THE BEST SHORT STORIES OF 1930, ed. Edward J. O'Brien.   B2
New York: Dodd, Mead and Company, 1930.
Miss Porter contributed:
"Theft." Pp. 171-176.
    First appeared in The Gyroscope, November 1929.

1933

THE BEST SHORT STORIES OF 1933, ed. Edward J. O'Brien.   B3
New York: Houghton Mifflin Company, 1933.
Miss Porter contributed:
"The Cracked Looking-Glass." Pp. 223-253.
    First appeared in Scribner's Magazine, Vol. XCI, May
1932.

1936

THE BEST SHORT STORIES 1936, ed. Edward J. O'Brien.   B4
Boston: Houghton Mifflin Company, 1936.
Miss Porter contributed:
"The Grave." Pp. 245-250.
    First appeared in Virginia Quarterly Review, Vol. XI,
April 1935.

A BOOK OF CONTEMPORARY SHORT STORIES, ed. Dorothy   B5
Brewster. New York: The Macmillan Company, 1936.
Miss Porter contributed:
"Maria Concepción." Pp. 249-272.
    First appeared in Century, Vol. CV, December 1922.

1937

HART CRANE, by Phillip Horton. New York: Norton &   B6
Company, 1937.

Mr. Horton says, "In some random recollections..., written in
later years, Miss Porter left an eloquent record of Crane's
spiritual disorder and anguish," which he quotes on pp. 285-287.

MODERN SHORT STORIES, ed. L. Brown. New York: B7
Harcourt, Brace and Company, 1937.
Miss Porter contributed:
"Maria Concepción." Pp. 615-640.
    First appeared in Century, Vol. CV, December 1922.

A SOUTHERN HARVEST, ed. Robert Penn Warren. Boston: B8
Houghton Mifflin Company, 1937.
Miss Porter contributed:
"He." Pp. 21-31.
    First appeared in New Masses, Vol. III, October 1927.

SOUTHERN TREASURY OF LIFE AND LITERATURE,   B9
selected by Stark Young, author's edition. New York:
Charles Scribner's Sons, 1937.
Miss Porter contributed:
"The Grave." Pp. 707-713.
    First appeared in Virginia Quarterly Review, Vol. XI,
    April 1935.

1938

WRITERS TAKE SIDES: LETTERS ABOUT THE WAR IN   B10
SPAIN FROM 418 AMERICAN AUTHORS. New York: League
of American Writers, 1938.
Miss Porter contributed a letter. P. 47.

1939

TELLERS OF TALES: 100 Short Stories from the United   B11
States, England, France, Russia and Germany, selected and

with an introduction by W. Somerset Maugham. New York:
Doubleday, Doran & Company, 1939.
Miss Porter contributed:
"Maria Concepción." Pp. 1390-1405.
First appeared in Century, Vol. CV, December 1922.

1940

THE BEST SHORT STORIES 1940, ed. Edward J. O'Brien.   B12
Boston: Houghton Mifflin Company, 1940.
Miss Porter contributed:
"The Downward Path to Wisdom." Pp. 311-332.
        First appeared in Harper's Bazaar, Vol. MMDCCXXXI,
        December 1939.

NEW DIRECTIONS IN PROSE AND POETRY, ed. James   B13
Laughlin. Norfolk, Connecticut: New Directions, 1940.
Miss Porter contributed:
"Notes on Writing." Pp. 195-204. (In "Notes on Contributors,"
p. ix, the editor states: "The notes which we print here are
excerpts from her [Miss Porter's] Journal, a record kept during
the years when she was living abroad in Germany, Switzerland,
and France.")
        First appeared here.

O. HENRY MEMORIAL AWARD PRIZE STORIES OF 1940,   B14
selected and edited by Harry Hansen. New York: Doubleday,
Doran & Company, Inc., 1940.
Miss Porter contributed:
"The Downward Path to Wisdom." Pp. 209-235.
        First appeared in Harper's Bazaar, Vol. MMDCCXXXI,
        December, 1939.

1941

A CURTAIN OF GREEN AND OTHER STORIES, by Eudora   B15
Welty. New York: Harcourt, Brace and Company, 1941.
Printing identified by "B.5.57" on copyright page.

Miss Porter contributed:

"Introduction. " Pp. xi-xxiii.

First appeared here.

HERE WE ARE: Stories from Scholastic magazine, ed.   B16

E.K. Taggard.   New York: Robert M. McBride & Company,

1941.

Miss Porter contributed:

"Rope. " Pp. 219-232.

First appeared in The Second American Caravan, ed.

A. Kreymborg. New York: The Macaulay Co., 1928.

INVITATION TO LEARNING, ed. Huntington Cairns, Allen   B17

Tate, and Mark Van Doren. New York: Random House, 1941.

First printing.

On one of a series of programs broadcast by the Columbia

Broadcasting System, Miss Porter, in an unrehearsed dialogue,

discussed Daniel Defoe's Moll Flanders with Mr. Cairns, Mr.

Tate, and Mr. Van Doren. Invitation to Learning contains a

transcript of this discussion made from a direct recording.

First appeared in print here. Pp. 137-151.

1942

AMERICAN HARVEST: TWENTY YEARS OF CREATIVE   B18

WRITING IN THE UNITED STATES, ed. Allen Tate and John

Peale Bishop. New York: L.B. Fischer Company, 1942.

Miss Porter contributed:

"Flowering Judas. " Pp. 488-502.

First appeared in Hound and Horn, Vol. III, Spring 1930.

INVITATION TO LEARNING, ed. Huntington Cairns, Allen   B19

Tate, and Mark Van Doren. New York: The New Home

Library, 1942.

The New Home Library edition of B17, published September

1942. Pp. 137-151.

First appeared in print in Invitation to Learning, ed.

Huntington Cairns, Allen Tate, and Mark Van Doren.
New York: Random House, 1941.

THE ITCHING PARROT, by José Joaquín Fernández de   B20
Lizárdi, translated from the Spanish by Katherine Anne Porter.
Garden City, New York: Doubleday, Doran & Company, Inc.,
1942.
First edition, 20 March 1942.
Miss Porter contributed the introduction.   Pp. xiii-xliii.
First appeared here.

NEW DIRECTIONS: NUMBER 7, dedicated "In Memoriam: B21
Ford Madox Ford, 1875-1939," ed. James Laughlin.   Norfolk,
Connecticut: New Directions, 1942.
Miss Porter contributed:
An untitled essay as part of a symposium entitled "Homage to
Ford Madox Ford" by twenty-four authors.   Pp. 478-479.
First appeared here.

THE NEW INVITATION TO LEARNING, ed. Mark Van Doren.   B22
New York: Random House, 1942.
First printing.
On three of a series of programs broadcast by the Columbia
Broadcasting System, Miss Porter, in unrehearsed dialogues,
discussed first, Henry Fielding's Tom Jones with Allen Tate
and Mark Van Doren; second, Lewis Carroll's Alice in Wonder-
land with Bertrand Russell and Mr. Van Doren; and, third,
Henry James's The Turn of the Screw with Mr. Tate and Mr.
Van Doren.   The New Invitation to Learning contains trans-
scripts of these three programs on pp. 194-205, 208-220, and
223-235, respectively.
First appeared in print here.

READINGS FOR OUR TIMES, Vol. II, ed. Harold William   B23
Blodgett and Burges Johnson.   Boston: Ginn and Company, 1942.
Miss Porter contributed:

'Noon Wine." Pp. 143-182.

First appeared in Signatures, Vol. I, Spring 1936.

THIS IS MY BEST, from America's 93 Greatest Living   B24
Authors, ed. Whit Burnett and Burton C. Hoffman. New York:
The Dial Press, 1942.
Miss Porter contributed:
Her reasons for selecting "Flowering Judas" in an article en-
titled "Why She Selected 'Flowering Judas.'" Pp. 539-540.
The story itself follows on pp. 540-552.
> "Why She Selected 'Flowering Judas'" first appeared here.
> "Flowering Judas" first appeared in Hound and Horn, Vol.
> III, Spring 1930.

VOGUE'S FIRST READER (no editor given). New York: B25
Julian Messner, Incorporated, 1942.
Miss Porter contributed:
"Happy Land." Pp. 74-82.
'Now at Last a House of My Own." Pp. 289-294.
> "Happy Land" first appeared in Vogue, Vol. XCIV,
> 1 November 1939.
> 'Now at Last a House of My Own" first appeared in
> Vogue, 1 September 1941.

                              1943
ABOUT WOMEN, ed. H. Reed. Cleveland & New York: B26
World Publishing Company, 1943.
Miss Porter contributed:
"The Jilting of Granny Weatherall." Pp. 311-320.
> First appeared in transition, February 1929.

THE GREATEST STORIES OF ALL TIMES: TELLERS OF   B27
TALES, selected and with an introduction by William Somerset
Maugham. Garden City, New York: Garden City Publishing
Company, Inc., 1943.
A new edition of B11.

Miss Porter contributed:

"Maria Concepción." Pp. 1390-1405.

First appeared in Century, Vol. CV, December 1922.

INTRODUCTION TO MODERN ENGLISH AND AMERICAN   B28
LITERATURE, ed. W. S. Maugham. New York: New Home
Library, 1943.

Miss Porter contributed:

"Flowering Judas." Pp. 379-389.

First appeared in Hound and Horn, Spring 1930.

ROUNDUP TIME, ed. G.S. Perry. New York: McGraw-   B29
Hill Book Company, 1943. (Also London: Whittlessey House,
1943)

Miss Porter contributed:

"Maria Concepción." Pp. 25-45.

First appeared in Century Magazine, December 1922.

UNDERSTANDING FICTION, ed. Cleanth Brooks, Jr., and   B30
Robert Penn Warren. New York: Appleton-Century-Crofts,
Inc., 1943.

Miss Porter contributed:

"Old Mortality." Pp. 481-535.

First appeared in The Southern Review, Vol. II, Spring
1938.

1944

VOGUE'S FIRST READER, ed. F. Crowninshield. Garden   B31
City, New York: Halcyon House, 1944.

Miss Porter contributed:

"Happy Land." Pp. 74-82.

First appeared in Vogue, Vol. XCIV, 1 November 1939.

1945

MASTERS OF THE SHORT STORY, ed. Walter Havighurst.   B32
New York: Harcourt, Brace and Company, 1945.

Miss Porter contributed:

"Maria Concepción."   Pp. 409-432.

     First appeared in Century, Vol. CV, December 1922.

MID COUNTRY: WRITINGS FROM THE HEART OF AMER-   B33
ICA, ed. Lowry C. Wimberley with an introduction by B.A.
Botkin. New York: Thomas Crowell Company, 1945. ("Sole
distributors in the United States and Canada, University of
Nebraska Press, Lincoln, Nebraska.")
Miss Porter contributed:
"The Source."   Pp. 1-5.

     First appeared in Accent, Vol. I, Spring 1941.

modern american short stories [not capitalized], ed. Bennett   B34
Cerf. Cleveland: The World Publishing Company, 1945.
Miss Porter contributed:
"The Circus."   Pp. 175-180.

     First appeared in The Southern Review, Vol. I, July 1935.

NORTH, EAST, SOUTH, WEST: A REGIONAL ANTHOLOGY   B35
OF AMERICAN WRITING, ed. Charles Lee. New York:
Howell, Soskin, 1945.
Miss Porter contributed:
"The Grave."   Pp. 327-332.

     First appeared in Virginia Quarterly Review, Vol. XI,
     April 1935.

PRESENT TENSE, ed. Sharon Brown. New York: Harcourt,   B36
Brace and Company, 1945.
Revised edition.
Miss Porter contributed:
"A Day's Work."   Pp. 257-272.

     First appeared in Nation, Vol. CL, 10 February 1940.

READING I'VE LIKED, ed. Clifton Fadiman. New York: B37
Simon and Schuster, 1945.

Miss Porter contributed:

'Noon Wine." Pp. 775-824.

First appeared in Signatures, Vol. I, Spring 1936.

TIME TO BE YOUNG, Whit Burnett. New York: J.B.   B38
Lippincott Company, 1945.

Miss Porter contributed:

"The Downward Path to Wisdom." Pp. 103-119.

First appeared in Harper's Bazaar, December 1939.

1946

ACCENT ANTHOLOGY: SELECTIONS FROM ACCENT, a   B39
Quarterly of New Literature, 1940-1945, ed. Kerker Quinn
and Charles Shattuck. New York: Harcourt, Brace and Company, 1946.

First edition.

Miss Porter contributed:

"Affectation of Praehiminincies." Pp. 220-240.

> First appeared in Accent, Vol. II, Spring 1942 and
> Summer 1942.

GREAT AMERICAN SHORT NOVELS, ed. William Phillips.   B40
New York: The Dial Press, 1946.

Miss Porter contributed:

"Pale Horse, Pale Rider." Pp. 577-624.

> First appeared in The Southern Review, Vol. III, Winter
> 1938.

LADY'S PLEASURE, (no editor given in listing examined).   B41
(No place given): William Penn Publishing Co., 1946.

Miss Porter contributed:

'Rope." Pp. 180-187.

> First appeared in The Second American Caravan, ed. A.
> Kreymborg. New York: The Macaulay Co., 1928.

1947

AMERICAN POETRY AND PROSE, ed. Norman Foerster.   B42
Boston: Houghton Mifflin Company, 1947.
Third edition.
Miss Porter contributed:
"Maria Concepción." Pp. 1551-1561.
  First appeared in Century, Vol. CV, December 1922.

THE GOLDEN ARGOSY: A COLLECTION OF THE MOST   B43
CELEBRATED SHORT STORIES IN THE ENGLISH LANGUAGE,
ed. with comments by Charles Grayson and Van H. Cartmell.
New York: The Dial Press, 1947.
Miss Porter contributed:
"Flowering Judas." Pp. 510-520.
  First appeared in Hound and Horn, Vol. III, Spring 1930.

LITERATURE FOR OUR TIME: AN ANTHOLOGY FOR COL-   B44
LEGE FRESHMEN, ed. Leonard Stanley Brown, Harlow O.
Waite, and Benjamin P. Atkinson. New York: Henry Holt and
Company, 1947.
Miss Porter contributed:
"A Day's Work." Pp. 311-324.
  First appeared in Nation, Vol. CL, 10 February 1940.

LIVING AMERICAN LITERATURE: PANORAMA OF AMERI-   B45
CAN LITERATURE, Book One, ed. W. Tasker Witham.
New York: Stephen Daye Press, 1947.
Miss Porter contributed:
"A Day's Work." Pp. 842-850.
  First appeared in Nation, Vol. CL, 10 February 1940.

A TREASURY OF SHORT STORIES, ed. Bernardine Kielty.   B46
New York: Simon and Schuster, 1947.
Miss Porter contributed:
"The Old Order." Pp. 839-849.
  First appeared in The Southern Review, Vol. I, No. 3,

Winter 1936.

A WORLD OF GREAT STORIES, ed. Hiram Collins Haydn   B47
and John Cournos. New York: Crown Publishers, 1947.
Miss Porter contributed:
"A Day's Work." Pp. 103-117.
First appeared in Nation, Vol. CL, 10 February 1940.

1948

BETTER READING 2: LITERATURE, ed. Walter Blair and   B48
John C. Gerber. Chicago: Scott, Foresman and Company,
1948.
Miss Porter contributed:
"Flowering Judas." Pp. 395-405.
First appeared in Hound and Horn, Vol. III, Spring 1930.

CRAFT OF THE SHORT STORY, ed. Richard Aldrich Sum-   B49
mers. New York: Rinehart and Company, Inc., 1948.
Miss Porter contributed:
"Flowering Judas." Pp. 272-284.
First appeared in Hound and Horn, Vol. III, Spring 1930.

INTRODUCTION TO LITERATURE, Vol. II of Readings for   B50
Liberal Education, ed. Louis Glenn Locke. New York:
Rinehart and Company, Inc., 1948.
Miss Porter contributed:
"That Tree." Pp. 398-408.
        First appeared in Virginia Quarterly Review, Vol. X,
        July 1934.

A TREASURY OF SHORT STORIES, ed. Bernardine Kielty.   B51
New York: Simon and Schuster, 1948.
Miss Porter contributed:
"The Old Order." Pp. 839-849.
        First appeared in The Southern Review, Vol. I, No. 3,
        Winter 1936.

1949

AMERICAN LIFE IN LITERATURE, Vol. II, ed. Jay Broadus   B52
Hubbell. New York: Harper and Brothers Publishers, 1949.
Revised edition.
Miss Porter contributed:
"The Circus." Pp. 884-887.
    First appeared in The Southern Review, Vol. I, July 1935.

AMERICAN LITERATURE: AN ANTHOLOGY AND CRITICAL   B53
SURVEY SINCE 1900, selected and edited by Joe Lee Davis,
John T. Frederick, and Frank Luther Mott. New York:
Charles Scribner's Sons, 1949.
Miss Porter contributed:
"The Jilting of Granny Weatherall." Pp. 813-819.
    First appeared in transition, Vol. XV, February 1929.

AMERICAN LITERATURE: AN ANTHOLOGY AND CRITICAL   B54
SURVEY FROM 1860 TO THE PRESENT, Vol. II, selected and
edited by Joe Lee Davis, John T. Frederick, and Frank Luther
Mott. New York: Charles Scribner's Sons, 1949.
Miss Porter contributed:
"The Jilting of Granny Weatherall." Pp. 813-819.
    First appeared in transition, Vol. XV, February 1929.

ANTHOLOGY FOR BASIC COMMUNICATION, ed. Alan   B55
Swallow, Iris Pavey Gilmore, and Marian Huxoll Talmadge.
Denver: The University of Denver Press, 1949.
Miss Porter contributed:
"Theft." Pp. 317-320.
    First appeared in The Gyroscope, November 1929.

THE ART OF MODERN FICTION, ed. Ray Benedict West,   B56
Jr., and Robert Wooster Stallman. New York: Holt, Rinehart
and Winston, 1949.
Miss Porter contributed:
"Flowering Judas." Pp. 277-291.

First appeared in <u>Hound and Horn</u>, Vol. III, Spring 1930.

CONTEMPORARY TRENDS: AMERICAN LITERATURE SINCE   B57
1900, ed. John Herbert Nelson and Oscar Cargill.   New York:
The Macmillan Company, 1949.
Revised edition.
Miss Porter contributed:
"The Witness."   Pp. 1074-1076.
    First appeared in <u>The Leaning Tower</u>.   New York:
    Harcourt, Brace and Company, 1944.

THE CRITICAL READER, ed. Wallace Douglas, Roy Lamson,   B58
and Hallett Smith.   New York: W. W. Norton & Company, Inc.,
1949.
Miss Porter contributed:
"Noon Wine."   Pp. 346-399.
    First appeared in <u>Signatures</u>, Vol. I, Spring 1936.

A LITTLE TREASURY OF AMERICAN PROSE: THE MAJOR   B59
WRITERS FROM COLONIAL TIMES TO THE PRESENT DAY,
ed. with an introduction by George Mayberry.   New York:
Charles Scribner's Sons, 1949.
Miss Porter contributed:
"An Introduction to Flowering Judas."   Pp. 594-595.
    First appeared in <u>Flowering Judas and Other Stories</u>.
    New York: The Modern Library, 1940.

MODERN RHETORIC, with readings, ed. Cleanth Brooks and   B60
Robert Penn Warren.   New York: Harcourt, Brace and Com-
pany, 1949.
Miss Porter contributed:
An excerpt from "The Downward Path to Wisdom."   P. 232.
An excerpt from "Flowering Judas."   P. 241.
An excerpt from "Hacienda."   Pp. 461-462.
    "The Downward Path to Wisdom" first appeared in
    <u>Harper's Bazaar</u>, Vol. MMDCCXXXI, December 1939.

Contributions to Books

"Flowering Judas" first appeared in Hound and Horn,
Vol. III, Spring 1930.

"Hacienda" first appeared in Virginia Quarterly Review,
Vol. VIII, October 1932.

READINGS FOR OUR TIMES, VOL. II, ed. Harold William   B61
Blodgett and Burges Johnson, Boston: Ginn and Company,
1949.
Second edition.
Miss Porter contributed:
"Noon Wine." Pp. 141-180.
First appeared in Signatures, Vol. I, Spring 1936.

SHORT STORY CRAFT, ed. Warren Bower with "An Introduc- B62
tion to Short Story Writing" by Lillian Bernard Gilkes. New York:
The Macmillan Company, 1949.
Miss Porter contributed:
"Maria Concepción." Pp. 251-270.
First appeared in Century, Vol. CV, December 1922.

THIS GENERATION, ed. George K. Anderson and Eda Lou   B63
Walton. Chicago: Scott, Foresman and Company, 1949.
Revised edition.
Miss Porter contributed:
"A Day's Work." Pp. 323-333.
First appeared in Nation, Vol. CL, 10 February 1940.

TRANSITION WORKSHOP, ed. Eugene Jolas. New York: B64
The Vanguard Press, Inc., 1949.
Miss Porter contributed:
"Magic." Pp. 111-113.
First appeared in transition, Vol. XIII, Summer 1928.

VOGUE'S FIRST READER (no editor given). Garden City,   B65
New York: Halcyon House, 1949. On copyright page: "Halcyon
House Reprint Edition, 1949, by special arrangement with

Julian Messner, Inc. "

Miss Porter contributed:

"Happy Land. " Pp. 74-82.

'Now at Last a House of My Own. " Pp. 289-294.

> "Happy Land" first appeared in Vogue, Vol. XCIV,
> 1 November 1939.
>
> 'Now at Last a House of My Own" first appeared in
> Vogue, 1 September 1941.

1950

GREAT SHORT STORIES, ed. Wilbur Schramm. New York: B66
Harcourt, Brace and Company, 1950.

Miss Porter contributed:

"The Jilting of Granny Weatherall. " Pp. 289-298.

> First appeared in transition, Vol. XV, February 1929.

GREAT SHORT STORIES FROM THE WORLD'S LITERATURE,   B67
ed. Charles Neider. New York: Rinehart and Company, Inc.,
1950.

Miss Porter contributed:

"Flowering Judas. " Pp. 334-346.

> First appeared in Hound and Horn, Vol. III, Spring 1930.

THE HOUSE OF FICTION: An Anthology of the Short Story   B68
with commentary by Caroline Gordon and Allen Tate. New York:
Charles Scribner's Sons, 1950.

Miss Porter contributed:

"Old Mortality. " Pp. 445-482.

> First appeared in The Southern Review, Vol. II,
> Spring 1938.

MANY-COLORED FLEECE, ed. Sister Mariella Gable,   B69
O.S.B. New York: Sneed and Ward, 1950.

Miss Porter contributed:

"The Jilting of Granny Weatherall. " Pp. 286-297.

> First appeared in transition, Vol. XV, February 1929.

MODERN SHORT STORIES: A CRITICAL ANTHOLOGY, ed.   B70
Robert Bechtold Heilman. New York: Harcourt, Brace and
Company, 1950.
Another impression gives publication data "New York and Bur-
lingame: Harcourt, Brace and World, Inc., 1950," but page
numbers of story are identical with the preceding.
Miss Porter contributed:
"Flowering Judas." Pp. 180-192.
    First appeared in Hound and Horn, Vol. III, Spring 1930.

THE STORY: A CRITICAL ANTHOLOGY, ed. Mark Schorer.   B71
Englewood Cliffs, New Jersey: Prentice-Hall, 1950.
Miss Porter contributed:
"The Grave." Pp. 253-260.
    First appeared in Virginia Quarterly Review, Vol. XI,
    April 1935.

                                1951
THE COLLEGE OMNIBUS, ed. Leonard F. Dean. New York: B72
Harcourt, Brace and Company, 1951.
Seventh edition.
Miss Porter contributed:
"Pale Horse, Pale Rider." Pp. 472-506.
    First appeared in The Southern Review, Vol. III,
    Winter 1938.

LITERARY OPINION IN AMERICA, ed. Morton D. Zabel.   B73
New York: Harper and Brothers, 1951.
Miss Porter contributed:
"Gertrude Stein: a Self-Portrait." Pp. 338-350.
    First appeared in Harper's Magazine, Vol. CXCV,
    December 1947.

MODERN SHORT STORIES, ed. Marvin Felheim, Franklin B.   B74
Newman, and William R. Steinhoff. New York: Oxford University Press, 1951.

Miss Porter contributed:

"That Tree." Pp. 174-187.

First appeared in Virginia Quarterly Review, Vol. X,
July 1934.

WORLD'S BEST DOCTOR STORIES, ed. Noah D. Fabricant   B75
and Heinz Werner. Garden City, New York: Garden City Books,
1951.

Miss Porter contributed:

"The Jilting of Granny Weatherall." Pp. 209-219.

First appeared in transition, February 1929.

WRITING FROM OBSERVATION, The Department of English,   B76
Wayne University, revised under the editorship of George A.
Peck from the edition edited by Leslie L. Harrawalt and
Emilie A. Newcomb. New York: Harcourt, Brace and
Company, 1951.

Miss Porter contributed:

"Rope." Pp. 75-81.

First appeared in The Second American Caravan, ed. A.
Kreymborg. New York: Macaulay Company, 1928.

1952

AMERICAN POETRY AND PROSE, ed. Norman Foerster.   B77
Shorter edition, prepared with supplementary notes by William
Charvat. Boston: Houghton Mifflin Company, 1952.

Miss Porter contributed:

"Maria Concepción." Pp. 854-864.

First appeared in Century, Vol. CV, December 1922.

AN AMERICAN RHETORIC, William Whyte Watt. New York: B78
Rinehart and Company, Inc., 1952.

Miss Porter contributed:

Excerpts from "Pale Horse, Pale Rider." Pp. 175, 180, 197,
237.

"Pale Horse, Pale Rider" first appeared in The

Southern Review, Vol. III, Winter 1938.

american short stories, 1820 to the present [not capitalized],   B79
ed. Eugene Current-Garcia and Walton R. Patrick.   Chicago:
Scott, Foresman and Company, 1952.
Revised edition.
Miss Porter contributed:
"Flowering Judas. " Pp. 464-475.
First appeared in Hound and Horn, Vol. III, Spring 1930.

AN APPROACH TO LITERATURE, ed. Cleanth Brooks, John   B80
Thibaut Purser, and Robert Penn Warren. New York: Ap-
pleton-Century-Crofts, Inc., 1952.
Third edition.
Miss Porter contributed:
"Noon Wine. " Pp. 191-219.
First appeared in Signatures, Vol. I, Spring 1936.

INTRODUCTION TO LITERATURE, Vol. II of Readings for   B81
Liberal Education, ed. Louis Glenn Locke, William M. Gibson,
and George Arms. New York: Rinehart and Company, Inc.,
1952.
Revised edition.
Miss Porter contributed:
"That Tree. " Pp. 413-423.
First appeared in Virginia Quarterly Review, Vol. X,
July 1934.

THE LITERATURE OF THE SOUTH, ed. Richmond C. Beatty, B82
Floyd C. Watkins, T.D. Young, and Randall Stewart. Chicago:
Scott, Foresman and Company, 1952.
Miss Porter contributed:
"He. " Pp. 857-864.
First appeared in New Masses, Vol. III, October 1927.

9 SHORT NOVELS, ed. Richard M. Ludwig and Marvin B.   B83

Perry, Jr. Boston: D.C. Heath and Company, 1952.
Miss Porter contributed:
'Noon Wine." Pp. 173-210.
   First appeared in Signatures, Vol. I, Spring 1936.

READING MODERN FICTION, 29 stories with study aids,   B84
selected and edited by Winifred C. Lynskey. New York:
Charles Scribner's Sons, 1952.
Miss Porter contributed:
"Maria Concepción." Pp. 420-435.
   First appeared in Century, Vol. CV, December 1922.

1953

AN ANTHOLOGY OF STORIES FROM THE SOUTHERN RE-   B85
VIEW, ed. Cleanth Brooks and Robert Penn Warren.   Baton
Rouge: Louisiana State University, 1953.
Miss Porter contributed:
'Old Mortality." Pp. 144-192.
   First appeared in The Southern Review, Vol. II,
   Spring 1938.

EXPANDING HORIZONS: A READER FOR ENGLISH COM-   B86
POSITION, ed. Ernest W. Kinne and Arnold P. Drew.
New York: The Odyssey Press, 1953.
First edition.
Miss Porter contributed:
"The Circus." Pp. 31-36.
   First appeared in The Southern Review, Vol. I, July 1935.

EYES OF BOYHOOD, ed. Clyde Brion Davis.   Philadelphia: B87
J.B. Lippincott, 1953.
Miss Porter contributed:
"The Downward Path to Wisdom." Pp. 178-197.
   First appeared in Harper's Bazaar, Vol. MMDCCXXXI,
   December 1939.

HARPER'S MAGAZINE READER: A Selection of Articles,   B88
Stories and Poems from Harper's Magazine. New York:
Bantam Books, 1953.
First edition.
Miss Porter contributed:
"Gertrude Stein: A Self-Portrait." Pp. 257-276.
   First appeared in Harper's Magazine, Vol. CXCV,
December 1947.

THE LITERATURE OF THE UNITED STATES, Vol. Two,   B89
ed. Walter Blair, Theodore Hornberger, and Randall Stewart.
Chicago: Scott, Foresman and Company, 1953.
Revised edition.
Miss Porter contributed:
"Flowering Judas." Pp. 1071-1077.
   First appeared in Hound and Horn, Vol. III, Spring 1930.

stories [not capitalized]: BRITISH AND AMERICAN, ed.   B90
Jack Barry Ludwig and W. Richard Poirier. Boston: Houghton
Mifflin Company, The Riverside Press, Cambridge, 1953.
Miss Porter contributed:
"Flowering Judas." Pp. 176-188.
   First appeared in Hound and Horn, Vol. III, Spring 1930.

1954
BETTER READING TWO: LITERATURE, ed. Walter Blair   B91
and John C. Gerber. Chicago: Scott, Foresman and Com-
pany, 1954.
Revised edition.
Miss Porter contributed:
"Flowering Judas." Pp. 413-423.
   First appeared in Hound and Horn, Vol. III, Spring 1930.

THE FRESHMAN AND HIS WORLD, ed. Don Marion Wolfe,   B92
Ruth A. Firor, and Thomas L. Donahue. Harrisburg, Pennsylvania: The Stackpole Company, September 16, 1954.

Fourth edition.

Miss Porter contributed:

Excerpts from "Maria Concepción." Pp. 442, 445, 449, 451.

> "Maria Concepción" first appeared in Century, Vol. CV,
> December 1922.

SELECTED STORIES OF EUDORA WELTY, containing all of   B93
A Curtain of Green and Other Stories and The Wide Net and
Other Stories, The Modern Library Edition. New York: The
Modern Library, 1954.

First Modern Library edition.

Miss Porter contributed:

"Introduction." Pp. xi-xxiii.

> First appeared as the introduction to Miss Welty's
> A Curtain of Green and Other Stories, 1941.

SHORT STORY MASTERPIECES, ed. Robert Penn Warren   B94
and Albert Erskine. New York: Dell Publishing Co., Inc.,
1954.

Miss Porter contributed:

"Flowering Judas." Pp. 384-397.

> First appeared in Hound and Horn, Vol. III, Spring 1930.

SIX GREAT MODERN SHORT NOVELS, (no editor given).   B95
New York: Dell Publishing Company, Inc., 1954.

Miss Porter contributed:

"Noon Wine." Pp. 155-212.

> First appeared in Signatures, Vol. I, Spring 1936.

21 TEXAS SHORT STORIES, ed. William Wallace Peery.   B96
Austin: University of Texas Press, 1954.

Miss Porter contributed:

"The Grave." Pp. 132-137.

> First appeared in Virginia Quarterly Review, Vol. XI,
> April 1935.

1955

AMERICA IN LITERATURE, ed. Tremaine McDowell. War   B97
Department Educational Manual EM612 published for the United
States Armed Forces Institute by F.S. Crofts and Company,
Inc., War Department, Washington 25, D.C., 4 April 1955.
Another issue of War Department Educational Manual EM612 is
in cloth with preliminary wartime explanations omitted (n.d.).
Text appears to be identical.
Miss Porter contributed:
"Rope." Pp. 387-392.

> First appeared in The Second American Caravan, ed. A.
> Kreymborg. New York: The Macaulay Company, 1928.

AMERICAN HERITAGE: AN ANTHOLOGY AND INTERPRE-   B98
TIVE SURVEY OF OUR LITERATURE, Vol. Two, ed. Leon
Howard, Louis B. Wright, and Carl Bode. Boston: D.C.
Heath and Company, 1955. (An Atlantic Monthly Press Book)
Miss Porter contributed:
"Theft." Pp. 780-783.

> First appeared in The Gyroscope, November 1929.

THE AMERICAN TREASURY 1455-1955, selected, arranged   B99
and edited by Clifton Fadiman, assisted by Charles Van Doren.
New York: Harper and Brothers, Publishers, 1955.
First edition.
Miss Porter contributed:
Brief excerpts from introduction to Flowering Judas and Other
Stories and from The Days Before. P. 954.

> First excerpt first appeared in Flowering Judas and
> Other Stories, New York: The Modern Library, 1940,
> pp. ix-x. Second excerpt first appeared in The Days
> Before, New York: Harcourt, Brace and Company, 1952.

A BOOK OF STORIES, ed. Royal Alfred Gettmann and Bruce   B100
Harkness. New York: Rinehart and Company, Inc., 1955.
Miss Porter contributed:

"Noon Wine." Pp. 393-441.

First appeared in Signatures, Vol. I, Spring 1936.

THE COLLEGE OMNIBUS, ed. Leonard F. Dean. New   B101
York: Harcourt, Brace and Company, 1955.
Eighth edition.
Miss Porter contributed:
"Pale Horse, Pale Rider." Pp. 551-585.

First appeared in The Southern Review, Vol. III,
Winter 1938.

MASTERS OF THE MODERN SHORT STORY, ed. Walter   B102
Havighurst. New York and Burlingame: Harcourt, Brace
and World, Inc., 1955.   (Library of Congress copy has "1954,
1955 by Harcourt, Brace and Company, Inc.," and has "a.10.
54" on copyright page; however, stamped date of copyright office is "January 12, 1955.")
A new edition.
Miss Porter contributed:
"The Jilting of Granny Weatherall." Pp. 234-244.

First appeared in transition, Vol. XV, February 1929.

PATTERNS FOR LIVING, ed. Oscar James Campbell. New   B103
York: The Macmillan Company, 1955.
Fourth edition.
Miss Porter contributed:
"Marriage Is Belonging." Pp. 163-166.

First appeared in Mademoiselle, Vol. XXXIII, October
1951.

READING MODERN SHORT STORIES, ed. Jarvis A. Thurs-   B104
ton, Chicago: Scott, Foresman and Company, 1955.
Miss Porter contributed:
"The Circus." Pp. 267-271.
"The Jilting of Granny Weatherall." Pp. 271-280.

"The Circus" first appeared in The Southern Review,

Vol. I, July 1935.

"The Jilting of Granny Weatherall" first appeared in
transition, Vol. XV, February 1929.

THE RETRIAL OF JOAN OF ARC, by Reginé Pernoud,   B105
translated by J. M. Cohen. New York: Harcourt, Brace and
Company, 1955.
First American edition.
Miss Porter contributed:
The Foreword. Pp. v-viii.
First appeared here.

SOUTHERN READER, ed. Willard Thorp. New York: B106
Alfred A. Knopf, 1955.
Miss Porter contributed:
"The Grave." Pp. 712-717.
First appeared in Virginia Quarterly Review, April 1935.

A TREASURY OF AMERICAN LITERATURE, Vol. II, from   B107
1860 to the present, selected and edited by Joe Lee Davis,
John T. Frederick, and Frank Luther Mott. Chicago:
Spencer Press, Charles Scribner's Sons, Inc., 1955.
Miss Porter contributed:
"The Jilting of Granny Weatherall." Pp. 813-819.
First appeared in transition, Vol. XV, February 1929.

1956
CRITICAL THINKING AND THE HUMANITIES, ed. James   B108
Adair Fisher, Sidney J. Black, and Margaret H. Daugherty.
Boston: Boston University Press, 1956.
Miss Porter contributed:
"Noon Wine." Pp. 595-650.
First appeared in Signatures, Vol. I, Spring 1936.

THE GROWTH OF AMERICAN LITERATURE: A CRITICAL   B109
AND HISTORICAL SURVEY, Vol. II, ed. Edwin Harrison Cady,

Frederick J. Hoffman, and Roy Harvey Pearce. New York:
American Book Company, 1956.
Miss Porter contributed:
"The Grave." Pp. 657-661.
>   First appeared in Virginia Quarterly Review, Vol. XI,
>   April 1935.

THE SHORT STORY, (with analytical comment), ed. James   B110
B. Hall and Joseph Langland. New York: The Macmillan
Company, 1956.
First printing.
Miss Porter contributed:
"Theft." Pp. 375-381.
>   First appeared in The Gyroscope, November 1929.

THEME AND FORM: AN INTRODUCTION TO LITERATURE, B111
ed. Monroe C. Beardsley, Robert W. Daniel, and Glenn Leggett. Englewood Cliffs, New Jersey: Prentice-Hall, Inc., 1956.
Miss Porter contributed:
"The Grave." Pp. 548-551.
>   First appeared in Virginia Quarterly Review, Vol. XI,
>   April 1935.

1957
AMERICAN POETRY AND PROSE, ed. Norman Foerster.   B112
Boston: Houghton Mifflin Company, 1957.
Shorter edition.
Miss Porter contributed:
"Maria Concepción." Pp. 1521-1530.
>   First appeared in Century, Vol. CV, December 1922.

AMERICAN POETRY AND PROSE: Part II: FROM WALT   B113
WHITMAN TO THE PRESENT, ed. Norman Foerster.
Boston: Houghton Mifflin Company, 1957.
Fourth edition, complete.
Miss Porter contributed:

"Maria Concepción." Pp. 1521-1530.

   First appeared in Century, Vol. CV, December 1922.

AN AMERICAN RHETORIC, William Whyte Watt. New York: B114
Rinehart and Company, Inc., 1957.
Revised edition.
Miss Porter contributed:
Excerpts from "Pale Horse, Pale Rider." Pp. 200, 205, 224,
and 270.
   "Pale Horse, Pale Rider" first appeared in The
   Southern Review, Vol. III, Winter 1938.

COMPOSITION: A COURSE IN WRITING AND RHETORIC,   B115
Richard M. Weaver. New York: Henry Holt and Company,
1957.
Miss Porter contributed:
An excerpt from "Hacienda." p. 258.
   "Hacienda" first appeared in Virginia Quarterly Review,
   Vol. VIII, October 1932.

INTRODUCTION TO LITERATURE, Vol. II of Readings for   B116
Liberal Education, ed. Louis Glenn Locke. New York:
Rinehart and Company, 1957.
Third edition.
Miss Porter contributed:
"That Tree." Pp. 406-416.
   First appeared in Virginia Quarterly Review, Vol. X,
   July 1934.

THE LITERATURE OF THE UNITED STATES, ed. Walter   B117
Blair, Theodore Hornberger, and Randall Stewart. Chicago:
Scott, Foresman and Company, 1957.
Single-volume edition.
Miss Porter contributed:
"Flowering Judas." Pp. 1194-1204.
   First appeared in Hound and Horn, Vol. III, Spring 1930.

MASTERS AND MASTERPIECES OF THE SHORT STORY,   B118
first series, ed. Joshua McClennen.   New York: Henry Holt
and Company, 1957.
Miss Porter contributed:
"The Jilting of Granny Weatherall. "   Pp. 189-192.
"Theft. "   Pp. 193-195.
   "The Jilting of Granny Weatherall" first appeared in
   transition, Vol. XV, February 1929.
   "Theft" first appeared in The Gyroscope, November 1929.

READING MODERN FICTION, 29 stories with study aids,   B119
selected and edited by Winifred C. Lynskey.   New York:
Charles Scribner's Sons, 1957.
Revised edition.
Miss Porter contributed:
"Maria Concepción. "   Pp. 420-435.
   First appeared in Century, Vol. CV, December 1922.

READINGS FOR COLLEGE ENGLISH, ed. John Conrad   B120
Bushman and Ernest G. Matthews.   New York: American
Book Company, 1957.
Second edition.
Miss Porter contributed:
"Portrait: Old South. "   Pp. 47-51, with questions for discussion.
   First appeared in Mademoiselle, Vol. XVIII, February 1944.

1958
THE ANCHOR BOOK OF STORIES, selected and with an   B121
introduction by Randall Jarrell.   Garden City, New York:
Doubleday Anchor Books, Doubleday and Company, Inc., 1958.
Miss Porter contributed:
"He. "   Pp. 140-150.
   First appeared in New Masses, Vol. III, October 1927.

THE ART OF THE ESSAY, ed. Leslie Fiedler.   New York: B122
Thomas Y. Crowell Company, 1958.

Miss Porter contributed:

"Audubon's Happy Land." Pp. 138-145.

First appeared in Vogue, Vol. XCIV, 1 November 1939.

COLLEGE READING, A Collection of Prose, Plays, and   B123
Poetry, ed. George William Sanderlin. Boston: D.C. Heath
and Company, 1958.

Second edition.

Miss Porter contributed:

"Marriage Is Belonging." Pp. 191-194.

First appeared in Mademoiselle, Vol. XXXIII, October 1951.

MODERN LITERARY CRITICISM: AN ANTHOLOGY, edited   B124
with an introduction by Irving Howe. Boston: Beacon Press,
Beacon Hill, 1958.

Miss Porter contributed:

"On a Criticism of Thomas Hardy." Pp. 299-309.

First appeared in The Southern Review, Vol. VI, Summer
1940.

READING FOR WRITING, ed. Arthur Mizener. New York: B125
Henry Holt and Company, 1958.

Miss Porter contributed:

"The Future Is Now." Pp. 44-48, with questions pp. 48-50 and
suggested topics for writing p. 50.

First appeared in Mademoiselle, Vol. XXXII, November
1950.

SHORT STORY MASTERPIECES, ed. Robert Penn Warren   B126
and Albert Erskine. New York: Dell Publishing Co., Inc.,
1958.

Laurel Edition no. 7864, a new Dell edition. First printing,
March 1958.

Miss Porter contributed:

"Flowering Judas." Pp. 384-397.

First appeared in Hound and Horn, Vol. III, Spring 1930.

UNDERSTANDING AND USING ENGLISH, by Newman Peter   B127
Birk and Genevieve B. Birk.   New York: The Odyssey Press,
Inc., 1958.

First printing of the third edition.

Miss Porter contributed:

An excerpt from "Noon Wine."   P. 136.

    "Noon Wine" first appeared in Signatures, Vol. I,
    Spring 1936.

1959

AMERICAN SHORT STORIES, ed. Ray B. West.   New York: B128
Thomas Y. Crowell Co., 1959.

Miss Porter contributed:

"The Grave."   Pp. 200-204.

    First appeared in Virginia Quarterly Review, Vol. XI,
    April 1935.

BETTER READING II: LITERATURE, ed. Walter Blair and   B129
John C. Gerber.   Chicago: Scott, Foresman and Company,
1959.

Third edition.

Miss Porter contributed:

"Flowering Judas."   Pp. 409-418.

    First appeared in Hound and Horn, Vol. III, Spring 1930.

BRITISH AND AMERICAN ESSAYS, 1905-1956, compiled by   B130
Carl L. Anderson and George Walton Williams.   A Holt-
Dryden book.   New York: Henry Holt and Company, 1959.

Miss Porter contributed:

"The Future Is Now."   Pp. 94-100.

    First appeared in Mademoiselle, Vol. XXXII, November
    1950.

A CASEBOOK ON HENRY JAMES'S 'THE TURN OF THE   B131
SCREW," ed. Gerald Willen.   New York: Thomas Y. Crowell
Company, 1959.

First printing, November 1959.

Contains a transcript of a discussion by Miss Porter, Allen
Tate, and Mark Van Doren of James's "The Turn of the Screw."
[Explained fully under B20.]

> First appeared in print in The New Invitation to Learn-
> ing, ed. Mark Van Doren. New York: Random House,
> 1942.

A COMPLETE COURSE IN FRESHMAN ENGLISH, ed. Harry   B132
Shaw, with chapters by Lousene G. Rousseau, Anne L. Corbitt,
S. I. Hayakawa, Ralph G. Nichols, and Leonard A. Stevens.
New York: Harper and Row, Publishers, 1959.
Fifth edition.
Miss Porter contributed:
"The Stories of Eudora Welty." Pp. 886-891.

> First appeared as "Introduction," A Curtain of Green
> and Other Stories by Eudora Welty. New York:
> Harcourt, Brace and Company, Inc., 1941.

GENTLEMEN, SCHOLARS AND SCOUNDRELS: A Treasury   B133
of the Best of Harper's Magazine from 1850 to the Present,
ed. Horace Knowles. New York: Harper and Brothers, copyright 1915 . . . 1959.
Miss Porter contributed:
"Gertrude Stein: A Self-Portrait." Pp. 279-294.

> First appeared in Harper's Magazine, Vol. CXCV,
> December 1947.

A RHETORIC CASE BOOK, ed. Francis Xavier Connolly.   B134
New York: Harcourt, Brace and Company, 1959.
Second edition.
Miss Porter contributed:
"St. Francisville." Pp. 612-617.

> First appeared as "Happy Land" in Vogue, Vol. XCIV,
> 1 November 1939.

SHORT FICTION: A CRITICAL COLLECTION, ed. James   B135
R. Frakes and Isadore Traschen. Englewood Cliffs, New
Jersey: Prentice-Hall, Inc., 1959.
Miss Porter contributed:
"The Jilting of Granny Weatherall." Pp. 262-268.
    First appeared in transition, Vol. XV, February 1929.

SHORT STORY MASTERPIECES, ed. Robert Penn Warren   B136
and Albert Erskine. New York: Dell Publishing Co., Inc.,
1959.
Laurel Edition no. 7864, a new Dell edition. Second printing,
May 1959.
Miss Porter contributed:
"Flowering Judas." Pp. 384-397.
    First appeared in Hound and Horn, Vol. III, Spring 1930.

UNDERSTANDING AND USING ENGLISH, by Newman Peter   B137
Birk and Genevieve B. Birk. New York: The Odyssey Press,
Inc., 1959.
Third edition with readings.
Miss Porter contributed:
An excerpt from "Noon Wine." P. 136.
        "Noon Wine" first appeared in Signatures, Vol. I,
        Spring 1936.

UNDERSTANDING FICTION, Cleanth Brooks and Robert Penn B138
Warren. New York: Appleton-Century-Crofts, Inc., 1959.
Second edition.
Miss Porter contributed:
"Noon Wine." Pp. 573-610.
"'Noon Wine': The Sources." Pp. 610-620.
        "Noon Wine" first appeared in Signatures, Vol. I,
        Spring 1936.
        "'Noon Wine': The Sources" first appeared in Yale
        Review, Vol. XLVI, 1 September 1956.

WRITING FROM OBSERVATION, The Department of English, B139
Wayne University, revised under the editorship of Lester W.
Cameron and Samuel A. Golden. New York: Harcourt,
Brace and Company, 1959.
Third edition.
Miss Porter contributed:
"Rope." Pp. 132-137.
> First appeared in The Second American Caravan, ed. A.
> Kreymborg. New York: The Macaulay Company, 1928.

1960

AMERICAN POETRY AND PROSE, ed. Norman Foerster and B140
Robert Falk. Boston: Houghton Mifflin Company, 1960.
New Shorter Edition. Abridged and revised from the Fourth
Edition, Complete, of American Poetry and Prose, ed.
Norman Foerster.
Miss Porter contributed:
"Maria Concepción." Pp. 1091-1100.
> First appeared in Century, Vol. CV, December 1922.

THE ART OF MODERN FICTION, ed. Ray B. West, Jr.   B141
and Robert Wooster Stallman. New York: Holt, Rinehart and
Winston, 1960.
Alternate edition. Copy seen was printed August 1960. Ac-
companying this edition was a teacher's manual with "Second
Printing, February 1960" on verso of copyright page.
Miss Porter contributed:
"Flowering Judas." Pp. 222-231.
> First appeared in Hound and Horn, Vol. III, Spring 1930.

BETTER READING: REPERTORY, ed. Walter Blair and   B142
John Gerber. Chicago: Scott, Foresman and Company, 1960.
Single-volume edition of BETTER READING ONE: FACTUAL
PROSE and BETTER READING TWO: LITERATURE.
Miss Porter contributed:
"Flowering Judas." Pp. 634-643.

First appeared in Hound and Horn, Vol. III, Spring 1930.

THE BRITANNICA LIBRARY OF GREAT AMERICAN WRIT-   B143
ING, Vol. II, edited with historical notes and a running com-
mentary by Louis Untermeyer. Chicago: Britannica Press
and distributed in association with J.B. Lippincott Company,
Philadelphia and New York, 1960.
Miss Porter contributed:
"The Old Order." Pp. 1502-1514.
        First appeared in The Southern Review, Vol. I,
        Winter 1936.

THE EXPERIENCE OF PROSE, ed. Walter Bates Rideout.   B144
New York: Thomas Y. Crowell Company, 1960.
Miss Porter contributed:
"Why I Write About Mexico." Pp. 142-144, with a letter to
the editor of the Century and an introductory sketch p. 142,
and questions p. 144.
        First appeared as a letter to the editor of Century
        Magazine, written in 1923.

FIFTY MODERN STORIES, ed. Thomas M.H. Blair.   B145
Evanston, Illinois: Row, Peterson and Company, 1960.
Miss Porter contributed:
"Theft." Pp. 565-570.
        First appeared in The Gyroscope, November 1929.

40 BEST STORIES FROM MADEMOISELLE 1935-1960, ed.   B146
Cyrilly Abels and Margarita G. Smith. New York: Harper
& Brothers, Publishers, 1960.
Miss Porter contributed:
"A Christmas Story." Pp. 75-79.
        First appeared in Mademoiselle, Vol. XXIV, December
        1946.

THE HOUSE OF FICTION: An Anthology of the Short Story,   B147

with commentary by Caroline Gordon and Allen Tate.
New York: Charles Scribner's Sons, 1960.
Second edition.
Miss Porter contributed:
"Old Mortality." Pp. 251-288.
First appeared in The Southern Review, Vol. II,
Spring 1938.

LITERARY TYPES AND THEMES, ed. Maurice B. McNamee, B148
James E. Cronin, and Joseph A. Rogers. New York: Holt,
Rinehart and Winston, Inc., 1960.
Miss Porter contributed:
"The Jilting of Granny Weatherall." Pp. 46-50.
First appeared in transition, Vol. XV, February 1929.

LITERATURE: AN INTRODUCTION, ed. Hollis Summers B149
and Edgar Whan. New York: McGraw-Hill Book Company,
Inc., 1960.
Miss Porter contributed:
"That Tree." Pp. 112-120.
First appeared in Virginia Quarterly Review, Vol. X,
July 1934.

MASTERS AND MASTERPIECES OF THE SHORT STORY, B150
second series, ed. Joshua McClennen. A Holt-Dryden Book.
New York: Henry Holt and Company, 1960.
Miss Porter contributed:
"Flowering Judas." Pp. 465-475.
"He." Pp. 475-483.
"Maria Concepción." Pp. 483-499.
    "Flowering Judas" first appeared in Hound and Horn,
    Vol. III, Spring 1930.
    "He" first appeared in New Masses, Vol. III, October 1927.
    "Maria Concepción" first appeared in Century, Vol. CV,
    December 1922.

REPERTORY: Single Volume Edition of Better Reading, ed.   B151
Walter Blair and John Gerber.   Chicago: Scott, Foresman
and Company, 1960.
Miss Porter contributed:
"Flowering Judas." Pp. 634-643.
First appeared in Hound and Horn, Vol. III, Spring 1930.

THE SCOPE OF FICTION, ed. Cleanth Brooks and Robert   B152
Penn Warren.   New York: Appleton-Century-Crofts, Inc.,
1960.
An abridgement of Understanding Fiction, second edition. (See B138)
Miss Porter contributed:
"Theft." Pp. 222-227.
First appeared in The Gyroscope, November 1929.

THE SHORT STORY AND THE READER, ed. Robert Stanton. B153
New York: Henry Holt and Company, 1960.
Miss Porter contributed:
"The Downward Path to Wisdom." Pp. 100-116.
First appeared in Harper's Bazaar, Vol. MMDCCXXXI,
December 1939.

SHORT STORY MASTERPIECES, ed. Robert Penn Warren   B154
and Albert Erskine.   New York: Dell Publishing Co., Inc.,
1960.
Laurel Edition no. 7864, a new Dell edition.
Miss Porter contributed:
"Flowering Judas." Pp. 384-397.
First appeared in Hound and Horn, Vol. III, Spring 1930.

31 STORIES, ed. Michael R. Booth and Clinton S. Burhans,   B155
Jr.   Englewood Cliffs, New Jersey: Prentice-Hall, Inc., 1960.
Miss Porter contributed:
"Theft." Pp. 212-217.
First appeared in The Gyroscope, November 1929.

1961

THE AMERICAN LITERARY RECORD, ed. Willard Thorp,   B156
Carlos Baker, James K. Falsom, and Merle Curti.   Chicago:
J.B. Lippincott Company, 1961.
Miss Porter contributed:
"The Grave." Pp. 907-910.
First appeared in Virginia Quarterly Review, Vol. XI,
April 1935.

AMERICAN LITERATURE: A COLLEGE SURVEY, ed.   B157
Clarence Arthur Brown and John T. Flanagan. New York:
McGraw-Hill Book Company, 1961.
Miss Porter contributed:
"The Jilting of Granny Weatherall." Pp. 711-715.
First appeared in transition, Vol. XV, February 1929.

THE AMERICAN TRADITION IN LITERATURE, Vol. II, ed.   B158
Sculley Bradley, Richmond Croom Beatty, and E. Hudson Long.
New York: W.W. Norton and Company, Inc., 1961.
Revised edition.
Miss Porter contributed:
"The Jilting of Granny Weatherall." Pp. 1250-1259.
First appeared in transition, Vol. XV, February 1929.

THE AMERICAN TRADITION IN LITERATURE, ed. Sculley   B159
Bradley, Richmond Croom Beatty, and E. Hudson Long.
New York: W.W. Norton and Company, Inc., 1961.
Revised edition in one volume.
Miss Porter contributed:
"The Jilting of Granny Weatherall." Pp. 1483-1491.
First appeared in transition, Vol. XV, February 1929.

A COLLEGE BOOK OF MODERN FICTION, ed. Walter B.   B160
Rideout and James K. Robinson. New York: Harper and Row
Publishers, 1961.
Miss Porter contributed:

"The Downward Path to Wisdom." Pp. 91-106.

    First appeared in Harper's Bazaar, Vol. MMDCCXXXI,
December 1939.

THE COMPLETE READER, ed. Richard S. Beal and Jacob   B161
Korg. Englewood Cliffs, New Jersey: Prentice-Hall, Inc.,
1961.
Miss Porter contributed:
"Theft." Pp. 174-179.

    First appeared in The Gyroscope, November 1929.

AN INTRODUCTION TO LITERATURE: FICTION, POETRY,   B162
DRAMA, ed. Sylvan Barnet, Morton Berman, and William
Burto. Boston: Little, Brown and Company, 1961.
Miss Porter contributed:
"The Jilting of Granny Weatherall." Pp. 207-214.

    First appeared in transition, February 1929.

SHORT STORIES: A STUDY IN PLEASURE, ed. Sean   B163
O'Faolain. Boston: Little, Brown and Company, 1961.
Miss Porter contributed:
"He." Pp. 254-264.

    First appeared in New Masses, Vol. III, October 1927.

STORIES OF MODERN AMERICA, ed. Herbert Gold and   B164
David L. Stevenson. New York: St [no period] Martin's
Press, 1961.
Miss Porter contributed:
"Flowering Judas." Pp. 294-306.

    First appeared in Hound and Horn, Vol. III, Spring 1930.

THE TROLL GARDEN, by Willa Cather. New York: B165
The New American Library, 1961.
"Signet Book" no. CD31.
Miss Porter contributed the afterword.

    First appeared here.

TWELVE SHORT STORIES, edited and with commentaries   B166
by Marvin Magalaner and Edmond L. Volpe. New York:
The Macmillan Company, 1961.
First printing.
Miss Porter contributed:
"Flowering Judas." Pp. 130-141.
First appeared in Hound and Horn, Vol. III, Spring 1930.

WHAT IS THE SHORT STORY? Case studies in the develop- B167
ment of a literary form, ed. Eugene Current-Garcia and
Walton R. Patrick. Chicago: Scott, Foresman and Com-
pany, 1961.
Miss Porter contributed:
"Theft." Pp. 383-388.
First appeared in The Gyroscope, November 1929.

1962
ANGLES OF VISION: READINGS IN THOUGHT AND OPIN-   B168
ION, ed. Edward Huberman and Robert R. Raymo. Boston:
Houghton Mifflin Company, 1962.
Miss Porter contributed:
"The Necessary Enemy." Pp. 211-214.
First appeared as "Love and Hate" in Mademoiselle,
October 1948.

AN APPROACH TO THE NOVEL, Realism and Romanticism   B169
in Fiction, ed. Eugene Current-Garcia and Walton R. Patrick.
Chicago: Scott, Foresman and Company, 1962.
Miss Porter contributed:
"Noon Wine." Pp. 445-486.
First appeared in Signatures, Vol. I, Spring 1936.

THE CRITICAL READER, ed. Roy Lamson, Hallett Smith,   B170
Hugh N. Maclean, and Wallace W. Douglas. New York:
W.W. Norton and Company, Inc., 1962.
Revised edition.

Miss Porter contributed:

'Noon Wine. " Pp. 438-491.

> First appeared in Signatures, Vol. I, Spring 1936.

THE FORMS OF FICTION, ed. John Champlin Gardner and   B171
Lennis Dunlap. New York: Random House, 1962.
First printing.
Miss Porter contributed:
"The Witness. " Pp. 38-40.

> First appeared in The Leaning Tower. New York:
> Harcourt, Brace and Company, 1944.

INTRODUCTION TO LITERATURE, Vol. II of Readings for   B172
Liberal Education, ed. Louis Glenn Locke, William M. Gibson,
and George Arms. New York: Rinehart and Company, 19
April 1962.
Fourth edition. Another printing gives publisher on title page
as Holt, Rinehart and Winston.
Miss Porter contributed:
"That Tree. " Pp. 408-418.

> First appeared in Virginia Quarterly Review, Vol. X,
> July 1934.

INTRODUCTION TO THE SHORT STORY: AN ANTHOLOGY   B173
(with questions at end), ed. Rocco Fumento. New York:
The Ronald Press Company, 1962.
Miss Porter contributed:
'Old Mortality. " Pp. 367-410.

> First appeared in The Southern Review, Vol. II,
> Spring 1938.

LITERATURE FOR WRITING: AN ANTHOLOGY OF MAJOR   B174
BRITISH AND AMERICAN AUTHORS, ed. Martin Steinmann,
Jr., and Gerald Willen. Belmont, California: Wadsworth
Publishing Company, Inc., 1962.
Miss Porter contributed:

"Flowering Judas." Pp. 177-183.

First appeared in Hound and Horn, Vol. III, Spring 1930.

LITERATURE: IDEA AND IMAGE, Vol. 2, Reading for   B175
College English, ed. Hans Paul Guth. Belmont, California:
Wadsworth Publishing Company, Inc., 1962.
First printing June 1962, second printing July 1963.
Miss Porter contributed:
"The Jilting of Granny Weatherall." Pp. 58-66.

First appeared in transition, Vol. XV, February 1929.

LOGIC AND RHETORIC, by James William Johnson.   B176
New York: The Macmillan Company, 1962.
First printing.
Miss Porter contributed:
"The Future Is Now." Pp. 154-159, with questions for dis-
cussion p. 159.

First appeared in Mademoiselle, Vol. XXXII, November
1950.

MODERN ESSAYS: A RHETORICAL APPROACH, ed. James   B177
G. Hepburn and Robert A. Greenberg. New York: The
Macmillan Company, 1962.
Miss Porter contributed:
"Audubon's Happy Land." Pp. 246-255.

First appeared in Vogue, Vol. XCIV, 1 November 1939.

MODERN SHORT STORIES; the fiction of experience [sic],   B178
ed. M.X. Lesser and John N. Morris. New York: McGraw-
Hill Book Company, Inc., 1962.
Miss Porter contributed:
"The Downward Path to Wisdom." Pp. 2-19.

First appeared in Harper's Bazaar, Vol. MMDCCXXXI,
December 1939.

MODERN SHORT STORIES: THE USES OF IMAGINATION,   B179

ed. Arthur Mizener. New York: W.W. Norton and Company,
Inc., 1962.

First edition.

Miss Porter contributed:

"The Grave." Pp. 113-119.

First appeared in Virginia Quarterly Review, Vol. XI,
April 1935.

PRIZE STORIES 1962: THE O. HENRY AWARDS, edited   B180
and with an introduction by Richard Poirier. Garden City,
New York: Doubleday & Company, Inc., 1962.

Miss Porter contributed:

"Holiday." Pp. 19-47.

First appeared in Atlantic Monthly, Vol. CCVI,
December 1960.

A READER FOR WRITERS: A CRITICAL ANTHOLOGY OF   B181
PROSE READINGS, ed. Jerome Walter Archer and Joseph
Schwartz. New York: McGraw-Hill Book Company, Inc.,
1962.

Miss Porter contributed:

"Portrait: Old South." Pp. 409-413, with questions for
discussion pp. 413-414.

First appeared in Mademoiselle, Vol. XVIII, February
1944.

READING MODERN FICTION, 29 stories with study aids,   B182
selected and edited by Winifred C. Lynskey. New York:
Charles Scribner's Sons, 1962.

Third edition.

Miss Porter contributed:

"Maria Concepción." Pp. 435-450.

First appeared in Century, Vol. CV, December 1922.

READINGS FOR RHETORIC: APPLICATIONS TO WRITING,   B183
ed. Caroline Shrodes, Clifford Josephson, and James R.

Wilson. New York: The Macmillan Company, 1962.

First printing.

Miss Porter contributed:

"The Wooden Umbrella." Pp. 426-440, with study helps and
writing suggestions, pp. 441-443.

> First appeared in Harper's Magazine, Vol. CXCV,
> December 1947, under the title of "Gertrude Stein:
> A self-Portrait."

REALISM AND ROMANTICISM IN FICTION, ed. Eugene   B184
Current-Garcia and Walton R. Patrick. Chicago: Scott,
Foresman and Company, 1962.

Miss Porter contributed:

'Noon Wine." Pp. 445-486.

> First appeared in Signatures, Vol. I, Spring 1936.

SHORT STORY MASTERPIECES, ed. Robert Penn Warren   B185
and Albert Erskine. New York: Dell Publishing Co., Inc.,
1962.

Laurel Edition no. 7864, a new Dell edition.

Miss Porter contributed:

"Flowering Judas." Pp. 384-397.

> First appeared in Hound and Horn, Vol. III, Spring 1930.

THEME AND FORM: AN INTRODUCTION TO LITERATURE, B186
ed. Monroe C. Beardsley, Robert W. Daniel, and Glenn
Leggett. Englewood Cliffs, New Jersey: Prentice-Hall, Inc.,
1962.

Second edition.

Miss Porter contributed:

"The Grave." Pp. 519-522.

> First appeared in Virginia Quarterly Review, Vol. XI,
> April 1935.

TWO AND TWENTY: A COLLECTION OF SHORT STORIES, B187
ed. Ralph H. Singleton. New York: St. Martin's Press, 1962.

Miss Porter contributed:

"The Circus." Pp. 258-264.

First appeared in The Southern Review, Vol. I, July 1935.

TYPES OF SHORT FICTION, ed. Roy R. Male. Belmont,   B188
California: Wadsworth Publishing Company, Inc., 1962.
Miss Porter contributed:

"That Tree." Pp. 174-187.

First appeared in Virginia Quarterly Review, Vol. X,
July 1934.

THE VILLAGE VOICE READER: A MIXED BAG FROM THE   B189
GREENWICH VILLAGE NEWSPAPER, ed. Daniel Wolf and
Edwin Fancher. Garden City, New York: Doubleday and
Company, Inc., 1962.
Miss Porter contributed:

"Romany Marie, Joe Gould--Two Legends Come to Life."
Pp. 252-255.

First appeared in The Village Voice, Vol. II, 11 September 1962.

THE WORLD OF SHORT FICTION: AN INTERNATIONAL   B190
COLLECTION, ed. Thomas A. Gullason and Leonard Casper.
New York: Harper and Row Publishers, Inc., 1962.
Miss Porter contributed:

"The Grave." Pp. 262-269.

"Flowering Judas." Pp. 270-284.

"The Grave" first appeared in Virginia Quarterly Review, Vol. XI, April 1935.

"Flowering Judas" first appeared in Hound and Horn,
Vol. III, Spring 1930.

1963

AN ANTHOLOGY OF FAMOUS AMERICAN STORIES, ed. by   B191
Angus Burrell and Bennett Cerf. New York: Random House,
Inc., 1962. (This book was copyrighted by The Modern Li-

brary, Inc., in 1936 and by Random House, Inc., in 1939, 1953, and 1963. A note following biographical entries at the end of the book states, "These biographical sketches have been revised in August, 1953. [signed] THE EDITORS." Thus the copy examined was apparently the revised edition of 1953 printed under a 1963 copyright, though this was not stated anywhere on either recto or verso of title page.)
Miss Porter contributed:
"Maria Concepción." Pp. 1024-1039.

First appeared in Century, Vol. CV, December 1922.

BENNETT CERF'S TAKE ALONG TREASURY, ed. Leonora   B192
Hornblow and Bennett Cerf. Garden City, New York:
Doubleday and Company, Inc., 1963.
First edition.
Miss Porter contributed:
"The Jilting of Granny Weatherall." Pp. 351-359.

First appeared in transition, Vol. XV, February 1929.

A COLLEGE FORUM, ed. Joseph Doggett, Everett Gillis,   B193
and Rosa Bludworth. New York: The Odyssey Press, Inc.,
1963.
Miss Porter contributed:
"The Jilting of Granny Weatherall." Pp. 589-597.

First appeared in transition, Vol. XV, February 1929.

ENGLISH ONE: A COMPLETE FRESHMAN COURSE, ed.   B194
Ray Frazer and Harold D. Kelling. Boston: D.C. Heath
and Company, 1963.
Miss Porter contributed:
"Theft." Pp. 308-312.

First appeared in The Gyroscope, November 1929.

THE EXPANDED MOMENT: A SHORT STORY ANTHOLOGY, B195
ed. Robert Coningsby Gordon. Boston: D.C. Heath and
Company, 1963.

Miss Porter contributed:

"Theft." Pp. 113-119.

 First appeared in The Gyroscope, November 1929.

FIRST-PRIZE STORIES FROM THE O. HENRY MEMORIAL B196
AWARDS, 1919-1966, ed. Harry Hansen. Garden City, New
York: Doubleday and Company, Inc., 1963.
Miss Porter contributed:

"Holiday." Pp. 646-669.

 First appeared in Atlantic Monthly, December 1960.

INTRODUCTION TO LITERATURE: STORIES, ed. Lynn B197
Altenbernd and Leslie L. Lewis. New York: The Macmillan
Company, 1963. This is a three-volume edition consisting
of Stories, Poems and Plays.
Miss Porter contributed:

"The Grave." Pp. 327-330.

  First appeared in Virginia Quarterly Review, Vol. XI,
  April 1935.

AN INTRODUCTION TO LITERATURE, ed. Sylvan Barnet, B198
Morton Berman, and William Burto. Boston: Little, Brown
and Company, 1963.
Second edition.
Miss Porter contributed:

"The Jilting of Granny Weatherall." Pp. 220-228.

 First appeared in transition, Vol. XV, February 1929.

THE LITERATURE OF THE UNITED STATES, ed. Walter B199
Blair, Theodore Hornberger and Randall Stewart. Chicago:
Scott, Foresman and Company, 1963.
Short edition.
Miss Porter contributed:

"Flowering Judas." Pp. 505-511.

 First appeared in Hound and Horn, Vol. III, Spring 1930.

TWENTY-THREE MODERN STORIES, ed. Barbara Howes.   B200
New York: Vintage Books, a division of Random House,
1963. (Vintage Books are published by Alfred A. Knopf, Inc.,
and Random House, Inc.)
First Vintage edition, February 1963.
Miss Porter contributed:
"Holiday." Pp. 55-86.
> First appeared in Atlantic Monthly, Vol. CCVI,
> December 1960. "Holiday" was copyrighted 1960
> by The Atlantic Monthly Company.

THE UNITED STATES IN LITERATURE, ed. Walter Blair,   B201
Paul Farmer, Theodore Hornberger, and Margaret Wasson.
Chicago: Scott, Foresman and Company, 1963.
Miss Porter contributed:
"The Jilting of Granny Weatherall." Pp. 468-473.
> First appeared in transition, Vol. XV, February 1929.

WHEN WOMEN LOOK AT MEN: AN ANTHOLOGY, ed.   B202
John Ahee Kouwenhoven and Janice Farrar Thaddeus. New
York: Harper and Row, 1963.
First edition.
Miss Porter contributed:
"A Day's Work." Pp. 390-407.
> First appeared in Nation, Vol. CL, 10 February 1940.

WRITING ABOUT LITERATURE, ed. B. Bernard Cohen.   B203
Chicago: Scott, Foresman and Company, 1963.
Miss Porter contributed:
"Flowering Judas." Pp. 167-178.
> First appeared in Hound and Horn, Vol. III, Spring 1930.

1964

AN AMERICAN RHETORIC, William Whyte Watt. New York: B204
Holt, Rinehart and Winston, 1964.
Third edition.

Miss Porter contributed:

Excerpts from "Pale Horse, Pale Rider." Pp. 185, 508
and 513.

"Pale Horse, Pale Rider" first appeared in The
Southern Review, Vol. III, Winter 1938.

american short stories, 1820 to the present [sic], ed.   B205
Eugene Current-Garcia and Walton R. Patrick. Chicago:
Scott, Foresman and Company, 1964.
Revised edition.
Miss Porter contributed:
"Flowering Judas." Pp. 424-435.

First appeared in Hound and Horn, Vol. III, Spring 1930.

AN APPROACH TO LITERATURE, by Cleanth Brooks,   B206
John Thibaut Purser and Robert Penn Warren. New York:
Appleton-Century-Crofts, 1964.
Fourth edition.
Miss Porter contributed:
'Noon Wine." Pp. 158-183.

First appeared in Signatures, Vol. I, Spring 1936.

THE DIMENSIONS OF THE SHORT STORY: A CRITICAL   B207
ANTHOLOGY, ed. James Edwin Miller, Jr., and Bernice
Slote. New York: Dodd, Mead and Company, 1964.
Miss Porter contributed:
"The Grave." Pp. 419-424.

First appeared in Virginia Quarterly Review, Vol. XI,
April 1935.

LITERATURE FOR WRITING: AN ANTHOLOGY OF MAJOR   B208
BRITISH AND AMERICAN AUTHORS, ed. Martin Steinmann,
Jr., and Gerald Willen. Belmont, California: Wadsworth
Publishing Company, Inc., 1964.
Miss Porter contributed:
"Flowering Judas." Pp. 177-184.

First appeared in <u>Hound and Horn</u>, Vol. III, Spring 1930.

MAN AND WARFARE: THEMATIC READINGS FOR COM-   B209
POSITION, ed. William F. Irmscher.   Boston: Little, Brown
and Company, 1964.
Miss Porter contributed:
"Pale Horse, Pale Rider." Pp. 289-335.
    First appeared in <u>The Southern Review</u>, Vol. III,
Winter 1938.

9 SHORT NOVELS, ed. Richard M. Ludwig and Marvin B.   B210
Perry, Jr. Boston: D.C. Heath and Company, 1964.
Second edition.
Miss Porter contributed:
"Noon Wine." Pp. 173-210.
    First appeared in <u>Signatures</u>, Vol. I, Spring 1936.

READING LITERATURE: PART II, ed. Joseph Henry Satin.   B211
Boston: Houghton Mifflin Company, 1964. This is Part II
of a four-volume edition consisting of Part I: <u>Reading Non-</u>
<u>Fiction Prose</u>; Part II: <u>Reading Prose Fiction</u>; Part III:
<u>Reading Drama</u>; Part IV: <u>Reading Poetry</u>.
Miss Porter contributed:
"Flowering Judas." Pp. 504-516.
    First appeared in <u>Hound and Horn</u>, Vol. III, Spring 1930.

THE RINEHART BOOK OF SHORT STORIES, ed. C.L.   B212
Cline. New York: Holt, Rinehart and Winston, Inc., 1964.
Alternate edition.
Miss Porter contributed:
"The Downward Path to Wisdom." Pp. 166-187.
    First appeared in <u>Harper's Bazaar</u>, Vol. MMDCCXXXI,
December 1939.

STORY: AN INTRODUCTION TO PROSE FICTION, ed.   B213
Arthur Foff and Daniel Knapp. Belmont, California:

Wadsworth Publishing Company, 1964.

Miss Porter contributed:

"Theft." Pp. 52-57.

> First appeared in The Gyroscope, November 1929.

1965

THE ART OF THE NOVELLA: EIGHT SHORT NOVELS,   B214
ed. Arnold B. Sklare and C.W. Post. New York: The
Macmillan Company, 1965.

Miss Porter contributed:

"Pale Horse, Pale Rider." Pp. 297-343.

> First appeared in The Southern Review, Vol. III,
> Winter 1938.

A COLLEGE BOOK OF AMERICAN LITERATURE, ed.   B215
Milton Ellis, Louise Pound, George Weida Spohn, and Frederick
J. Hoffman. New York: American Book Company, 1965.
Third edition.

Miss Porter contributed:

"The Jilting of Granny Weatherall." Pp. 1060-1065.

> First appeared in transition, Vol. XV, February 1929.

A COLLEGE BOOK OF AMERICAN LITERATURE, ed.   B216
Milton Ellis, Louise Pound, George Weida Spohn, and Frederick
J. Hoffman. New York: American Book Company, 1965.
Briefer course.

Miss Porter contributed:

"The Jilting of Granny Weatherall." Pp. 1058-1063.

> First appeared in transition, Vol. XV, February 1929.

THE MODERN NOVELETTE, ed. Ronald Paulson.   B217
Englewood Cliffs, New Jersey: Prentice-Hall, 1965.

Miss Porter contributed:

"Old Mortality." Pp. 285-319.

> First appeared in The Southern Review, Vol. II,
> Spring 1938.

PSYCHOPATHOLOGY AND LITERATURE, ed. Leslie Y.   B218
Rabkin. San Francisco: Chandler Publishing Company, 1965.
Miss Porter contributed:
"He." Pp. 270-281.
First appeared in New Masses, Vol. III, October 1927.

READ WITH ME, selected by Thomas Bertram Costain.   B219
New York: Doubleday and Company, Inc., 1965.
Miss Porter contributed:
"They Trample on Your Heart." Pp. 423-446.
This new title includes four of Miss Porter's stories
originally appearing as follows:
"The Source" first appeared in Accent, Spring 1931.
"The Witness" first appeared in The Leaning Tower
and Other Stories. New York: Harcourt, Brace and
Company, 1944.
"The Old Order" first appeared in The Southern Re-
view, Vol. I, Winter 1936.
"The Last Leaf" first appeared in The Leaning Tower
and Other Stories. New York: Harcourt, Brace and
Company, 1944.

THE REALM OF FICTION, ed. James B. Hall. New York: B220
McGraw-Hill Book Company, 1965.
Miss Porter contributed:
"Rope." Pp. 353-358.
First appeared in The Second American Caravan, ed. A.
Kreymborg. New York: Macaulay Company, 1928.

STUDIES IN CHANGE: A BOOK OF THE SHORT STORY,   B221
ed. Hugh Kenner. Englewood Cliffs, New Jersey: Prentice-
Hall, 1965.
Miss Porter contributed:
"The Grave." Pp. 18-23.
First appeared in Virginia Quarterly Review, Vol. XI,
April 1935.

TRIO: A BOOK OF STORIES, PLAYS, AND POEMS, ed.   B222
Harold P. Simonson. New York: Harper and Row, Pub-
lishers, Inc., 1965.
Second edition.
Miss Porter contributed:
"Flowering Judas." Pp. 115-126.
First appeared in Hound and Horn, Vol. III, Spring 1930.

1966

BETTER READING II: LITERATURE, ed. Walter Blair,   B223
John Gerber, and Eugene Garber. Chicago: Scott, Foresman
and Company, 1966.
Fourth edition.
Miss Porter contributed:
"Flowering Judas." Pp. 458-467.
First appeared in Hound and Horn, Vol. III, Spring 1930.

GREAT AMERICAN SHORT STORIES, ed. Wallace and Mary   B224
Stegner. New York: Dell Publishing Co., Inc., 1966.
Miss Porter contributed:
"He." Pp. 354-366.
First appeared in New Masses, Vol. III, October 1927.

AN INTRODUCTION TO LITERATURE, ed. Ralph H. Single-   B225
ton and Stanton Millet. New York: The World Publishing
Company, 1966.
Miss Porter contributed:
"The Circus." Pp. 434-438.
First appeared in The Southern Review, Vol. I, July 1935.

LITERATURE FOR UNDERSTANDING, ed. B. Bernard Cohen. B226
Chicago: Scott, Foresman and Company, 1966.
Miss Porter contributed:
"The Jilting of Granny Weatherall." Pp. 209-216.
First appeared in transition, Vol. XV, February 1929.

THE LITERATURE OF THE UNITED STATES, Vol. II,   B227
ed. Walter Blair, Theodore Hornberger, Randall Stewart,
and James E. Miller, Jr.   Chicago: Scott, Foresman and
Company, 1966.
Third edition.
Miss Porter contributed:
"Flowering Judas." Pp. 1195-1204.
> First appeared in Hound and Horn, Vol. III, Spring 1930.

A READER FOR WRITERS: A CRITICAL ANTHOLOGY OF   B228
PROSE READINGS, ed. Jerome W. Archer and Joseph
Schwartz. New York: McGraw-Hill Book Company, Inc., 1966.
Second edition.
Miss Porter contributed:
"Portrait: Old South." Pp. 440-444.
> First appeared in Mademoiselle, Vol. XVIII, February
> 1944.

THE SENSE OF FICTION, ed. Robert L. Welker and   B229
Herschel Gower. Englewood Cliffs, New Jersey: Prentice-
Hall, Inc., 1966.
Miss Porter contributed:
"The Grave." Pp. 145-149.
> First appeared in Virginia Quarterly Review, Vol. XI,
> April 1935.

THE SHORT STORY, ed. Willoughby Johnson and William C. B230
Hamlin. New York: American Book Co., 1966.
Miss Porter contributed:
"The Downward Path to Wisdom." Pp. 214-231.
> First appeared in Harper's Bazaar, Vol. MMDCCXXXI,
> December 1939.

SHORT STORY MASTERPIECES, ed. Robert Penn Warren   B231
and Albert Erskine. New York: Dell Publishing Co., Inc.,
1966.

Miss Porter contributed:

"Flowering Judas." Pp. 384-397.

   First appeared in Hound and Horn, Spring 1930.

THIRTEEN GREAT STORIES, ed. Daniel Talbot.   New York: B232
Dell Publishing Co., Inc., 1966.
Miss Porter contributed:
'The Downward Path to Wisdom." Pp. 71-89.

   First appeared in Harper's Bazaar, Vol. MMDCCXXXI,
   December 1939.

                              1967
THE ART OF FICTION: A HANDBOOK AND ANTHOLOGY,   B233
ed. R.F. Dietrich and Roger H. Sundell. New York: Holt,
Rinehart and Winston, Inc., 1967.
Miss Porter contributed:
"Flowering Judas." Pp. 412-422.

   First appeared in Hound and Horn, Vol. III, Spring 1930.

A COLLEGE FORUM, ed. Joseph Doggett, Everett Gillis,   B234
and Rosa Bludworth. New York: The Odyssey Press, Inc.,
1967.
Miss Porter contributed:
'The Jilting of Granny Weatherall." Pp. 589-597.

   First appeared in transition, Vol. XV, February 1929.

THE COMPLETE READER, ed. Richard S. Beal and Jacob   B235
Korg. Englewood Cliffs, New Jersey: Prentice-Hall, 1967.
Second edition.
Miss Porter contributed:
"Theft." Pp. 166-170.

   First appeared in The Gyroscope, November 1929.

THE FORMS OF FICTION, ed. John Gardner and Lennis   B236
Dunlap. New York: Random House, Inc., 1967.
Miss Porter contributed:

"The Witness."

   First appeared in The Leaning Tower and Other Stories.
   New York: Harcourt, Brace and Company, 1944.

GALAXY: LITERARY MODES AND GENRES, ed. Mark   B237
Schorer. New York: Harcourt, Brace and World, Inc., 1967.
Miss Porter contributed:
"He." Pp. 140-148.
   First appeared in New Masses, October 1927.

AN INTRODUCTION TO LITERATURE: FICTION, POETRY,   B238
DRAMA, ed. Sylvan Barnet, Morton Berman and William
Burto. Boston: Little, Brown and Company, 1967.
Third edition.
Miss Porter contributed:
"The Jilting of Granny Weatherall." Pp. 209-217.
   First appeared in transition, February 1929.

MASTERS OF THE MODERN SHORT STORY, ed. Walter E.   B239
Havighurst. New York: Harcourt, Brace and World, 1967.
Third edition.
Miss Porter contributed:
"The Jilting of Granny Weatherall." Pp. 234-244.
   First appeared in transition, February 1929.

MODERN SHORT STORIES: THE USES OF THE IMAGINA-   B240
TION, ed. Arthur Mizener. New York: W.W. Norton and
Company, Inc., 1967.
Revised edition.
Miss Porter contributed:
"The Grave." Pp. 149-155.
   First appeared in Virginia Quarterly Review, April 1935.

THE RANGE OF LITERATURE: AN INTRODUCTION TO   B241
PROSE AND VERSE, ed. Elisabeth W. Schneider, Albert L.
Walker, and Herbert E. Childs. New York: American Book

88 Katherine Anne Porter

Company, 1967.

Second edition.

Miss Porter contributed:

"Flowering Judas." Pp. 244-251.

First appeared in Hound and Horn, Vol. III, Spring 1930.

READING FOR RHETORIC: APPLICATIONS TO WRITING,   B242
ed. Caroline Shrodes, Clifford Josephson, and James R.
Wilson. New York: The Macmillan Company, 1967.

Second edition.

Miss Porter contributed:

"The Wooden Umbrella." Pp. 547-564.

First appeared in Harper's Magazine, December 1947,
under the title of "Gertrude Stein: A Self-Portrait."

THE SHAPE OF FICTION: BRITISH AND AMERICAN SHORT B243
STORIES, ed. Leo Hamalian and Frederick R. Karl. New
York: McGraw-Hill Book Company, 1967.

Miss Porter contributed:

"The Grave."

First appeared in Virginia Quarterly Review, April 1935.

THE SHAPE OF FICTION: STORIES FOR COMPARISON,   B244
ed. Alan Casty. Boston: D.C. Heath and Company, 1967.

Miss Porter contributed:

"Theft." Pp. 304-309.

First appeared in The Gyroscope, November 1929.

SHORT STORIES FOR INSIGHT, ed. Teresa Ferster Glazier. B245
New York: Harcourt, Brace and World, Inc., 1967.

Miss Porter contributed:

"Rope." Pp. 154-161.

First appeared in The Second American Caravan, ed. A.
Kreymborg. New York: The Macaulay Co., 1928.

THE SHORT STORY: An Inductive Approach, ed. Gerald   B246

Levin. New York: Harcourt, Brace and World, Inc., 1967.

Miss Porter contributed:

"Flowering Judas." Pp. 310-321.

    First appeared in Hound and Horn, Vol. III, Spring 1930.

THE STORY: A CRITICAL ANTHOLOGY, ed. Mark   B247
Schorer. Englewood Cliffs, New Jersey: Prentice-Hall, 1967.
Second edition.

Miss Porter contributed:

"The Grave." Pp. 208-213.

    First appeared in The Virginia Quarterly Review,
    April 1935.

1968

THE ART OF WRITING FICTION, ed. Ray B. West, Jr.   B248
New York: Thomas Y. Crowell Company, 1968.

Miss Porter contributed:

"Noon Wine." Pp. 21-66.

"'Noon Wine': The Sources." Pp. 67-80.

    "Noon Wine" first appeared in Signatures, Spring 1936.

    "'Noon Wine': The Sources" first appeared in the Yale
    Review, Vol. XLVI, 1 September 1956.

HERE AND NOW: AN APPROACH TO WRITING THROUGH   B249
PERCEPTION, ed. Fred Morgan. New York: Harcourt,
Brace and World, Inc., 1968.

Miss Porter contributed:

"The Witness." Pp. 95-97.

    First appeared in The Leaning Tower and Other Stories
    by Katherine Anne Porter. New York: Harcourt,
    Brace and Company, 1944.

THE LITERATURE OF THE SOUTH, ed. T.D. Young, Floyd   B250
C. Watkins, and Richmond Croom Beatty. Chicago: Scott,
Foresman and Company, 1968.
Revised edition.

Miss Porter contributed:

"He."   Pp. 826-833.

"The Grave."   Pp. 833-837.

> "He" first appeared in New Masses, October 1927.

> "The Grave" first appeared in Virginia Quarterly
> Review, April 1935.

MODERN ESSAYS: A RHETORICAL APPROACH, ed. James   B251
G. Hepburn and Robert A. Greenberg. New York: The
Macmillan Company, 1968.
Second edition.
Miss Porter contributed:

"Audubon's Happy Land."   Pp. 26-35.

> First appeared as "Happy Land" in Vogue, 1 November
> 1939.

MODERN SHORT STORIES: THE USES OF IMAGINATION,   B252
ed. Arthur Mizener. New York: W.W. Norton and Company, Inc., 1968.
Revised edition.
Miss Porter contributed:

"The Grave."   Pp. 149-155.

> First appeared in Virginia Quarterly Review, April 1935.

THE MODERN SHORT STORY, ed. Wilbur Huck and William   B253
Shanahan. Cincinnati: American Book Company, 1968.
Miss Porter contributed:

"Flowering Judas."   Pp. 104-114.

> First appeared in Hound and Horn, Spring 1930.

READING FOR UNDERSTANDING: FICTION, DRAMA,   B254
POETRY, ed. Caroline Shrodes, Joel Dorius, and Justine
Van Gundy. New York: The Macmillan Company, 1968.
Miss Porter contributed:

"Pale Horse, Pale Rider."   Pp. 417-466.

> First appeared in The Southern Review, Winter 1938.

READING MODERN FICTION, 31 Stories with Critical Aids,   B255
ed. Winifred Lynskey. New York: Charles Scribner's Sons,
1968.

Fourth edition.

Miss Porter contributed:

"Maria Concepción." Pp. 435-450.

First appeared in Century, Vol. CV, December 1922.

READINGS IN ENGLISH, ed. Dorothy W. Danielson and   B256
Rebecca E. Hayden. Englewood Cliffs, New Jersey:
Prentice-Hall, Inc., 1968.

Miss Porter contributed:

"The Jilting of Granny Weatherall." Pp. 115-124.

First appeared in transition, February 1929.

READING THE SHORT STORY, ed. Ray B. West, Jr.   B257
New York: Thomas Y. Crowell Company, 1968.

Miss Porter contributed:

"Noon Wine." Pp. 144-189.

"'Noon Wine': The Sources." Pp. 190-203.

"Noon Wine" first appeared in Signatures, Spring 1936.

"'Noon Wine': The Sources" first appeared in Yale
Review, Vol. XLVI, 1 September 1956.

STUDIES IN THE SHORT STORY, ed. Adrian H. Jaffe and   B258
Virgil Scott. New York: Holt, Rinehart and Winston, Inc.,
1968.

Third edition.

Miss Porter contributed:

"Flowering Judas."

First appeared in Hound and Horn, Vol. III, Spring 1930.

C. CONTRIBUTIONS TO PERIODICALS

1917

"The Week at the Theaters." The Critic and Camp Bowie   C1
Texahoma Bugler, Vol. III, No. 5, Fort Worth, Texas (January 12, 1917). Reviews by Miss Porter of four movies:
Until They Get Me; Empty Pockets, Herbert Brenon's screen
version of the novel by Rupert Hughes; The Judgment House,
written by Sir Gilbert Parker and produced by J. Stuart Black-
ton; and The Spirit of '17.

1920
"Adventures of Hadji." Asia, XX (August), pp. 683-684.   C2

1921
"The Mexican Trinity." The Freeman, III (August 3), pp. 493- C3
495.

1922
"Where Presidents Have No Friends." Century CIV (July),   C4
pp. 373-384.

"Maria Concepción." Century, CV (December), pp. 224-239.   C5

1923
"The Martyr." Century, CVI (July), pp. 410-413.   C6

[Letter to the Editor.] Century, CVI (July), [in contributor's   C7
section; pp. 8-10 (not numbered)].

"Enchanted" (poem). Literary Review, III (August 25), p. 921. C8

1924
"Two Songs from Mexico" (poems). The Measure: a Journal   C9
of Poetry, XXXV (January), p. 9.

"Requiescat" (poem). The Measure: a Journal of Poetry,   C10
XXXVIII (April), p. 11.

"Corridos." <u>Survey</u>, LII (May 1), pp. 157-159.   C11

"To a Portrait of the Poet" (translation of a poem by Sister   C12
Juana Inez de la Cruz). <u>Survey</u>, LII (May 1), p. 182.

"The Guild Spirit in American Art" (as told to Katherine   C13
Anne Porter by Diego Rivera). <u>Survey</u>, LII (May 1), pp. 174-
178.

"Mexico." <u>New York Tribune Books</u>, November 2, p. 9.   C14
        Reviews of <u>A Gringo in Mañana-Land</u>, by H.L. Foster,
        and <u>Beautiful Mexico</u>, by Vernon Quinn.

"A Self-Made Ghost." <u>New York Herald Tribune Books</u>,   C15
November 23, p. 3.
        Review of <u>The Triumph of Gallio</u>, by W.L. George.

"Virgin Violeta." <u>Century</u>, CIX (December), pp. 261-268.   C16

"The Poet and Her Imp." <u>New York Herald Tribune Books</u>,   C17
December 28, p. 3.
        Review of <u>Distressing Dialogues</u>, by Nancy Boyd
        (Edna St. Vincent Millay).

1925

"From a Mexican Painter's Notebooks" (translation from   C18
Diego Rivera's notebooks). <u>Arts</u>, VII (January), pp. 21-23.

"Maya Treasure." <u>New York Herald Tribune Books</u>, Febru-   C19
ary 8, p. 9.
        Review of <u>In an Unknown Land</u>, by Thomas Gann.

"Shooting the Shoots." <u>New York Herald Tribune Books</u>,   C20
March 8, p. 10.
        Reviews of <u>Round the World</u>, by F.H. Butler; <u>Outlines</u>
        <u>of Travel</u>, by Harman Black; and <u>My Trip Around the</u>

World, by Dorothy Dix.

"With the Enthusiasm of a Boy Scout." New York Herald   C21
Tribune Books, April 12, p. 10.
    Review of Adventures in Peru, by Cecil H. Prodgers.

"Over Adornment." New York Herald Tribune Books, July   C22
5, p. 12.
    Review of Ducdame, by John Cowper Powys.

"Sex and Civilization." New York Herald Tribune Books,   C23
July 5, pp. 3-4.
    Review of Our Changing Morality: A Symposium, ed.
    Freda Kerchway.

"The Complete Letter Writer." New Republic, XLIV   C24
(September 9), pp. 77-78.
    Review of Original Letters from India, by Eliza Fay
    (with a Foreword by E.M. Forster).

"Dora, the Dodo, and Utopia." New York Herald Tribune   C25
Books, November 8, p. 14.
    Reviews of Lysistrata, by A.M. Ludovici, and
    Hypatia, by Mrs. Bertrand Russell.

"Mr. George on the Woman Problem." New York Herald   C26
Tribune Books, November 29, p. 11.
    Review of The Story of Woman, by W.L. George.

"The Great Catherine." New York Herald Tribune Books,   C27
November 29, p. 3.
    Review of Catherine the Great, by Katherine Anthony.

"Etiquette in Action." New York Herald Tribune Books,   C28
December 20, p. 13.
    Review of Parade, by Emily Post.

"Ay, Que Chamaco." New Republic, XLV (December 23),   C29
pp. 141-142.
> Review of The Prince of Wales and Other Famous
> Americans: Caricatures, by Miguel Covarrubias.

1926

"Quetzalcoatl." New York Herald Tribune Books, March 7,   C30
p. 1.
> Review of The Plumed Serpent, by D.H. Lawrence.

"A Singing Woman." New York Herald Tribune Books, April   C31
18, p. 6.
> Review of Words for the Chisel, by Genevieve Taggard.

"La Conquistadora." New York Herald Tribune Books, April   C32
11, p. 3.
> Review of The Rosalie Evans Letters from Mexico,
> ed. D.C. Pettus.

"History for Boy and Girl Scouts." New Republic, XLVIII   C33
(November 10), p. 353.
> Review of Daniel Boone: Wilderness Scout, by
> S.E. White.

"Winter Burial" (poem). New York Herald Tribune Books,   C34
November 14, p. 2.

1927

"Everybody Is a Real One. New York Herald Tribune Books,   C35
January 16, pp. 1-2.
> A drawing of Miss Stein by Miss Porter and a review
> of The Making of Americans, by Gertrude Stein.

"Enthusiast and Wildcatter." New York Herald Tribune Books, C36
February 6, p. 14.
> Review of The City and the Sacred Well, by T.A. Willard.

"Children and Art." <u>Nation</u>, CXXIV (March 2), pp. 233-234.   C37

"Black, White, Red, Yellow and the Pintos." <u>New Republic</u>,   C38
L (March 16), pp. 111-112.
    Review of three books by R. B. Cunninghame Graham:
    The Ipane; Doughty Deeds: The Life of Robert Graham
    of Gartmore, 1735-1797; A Brazilian Mystic: The Life
    and Miracles of Antonio Conselheiro.

"Paternalism and the Mexican Problem." <u>New York Herald</u>   C39
<u>Tribune Books</u>, March 27.
    Reviews of <u>Some Mexican Problems</u>, by Moises Saenz
    and Herbert I. Priestly, and <u>Aspects of Mexican Civil-
    ization</u>, by Jose Vasconcelos and Manuel Gamio.

"A Philosopher at Court." <u>New York Herald Tribune Books</u>,   C40
August 14, p. 12.
    Review of <u>A Lady in Waiting to Queen Victoria,</u> by
    Magdalen Ponsonby.

"He." <u>New Masses</u>, III (October), pp. 13-15.   C41

"Semiramis Was a Good Girl." <u>New York Herald Tribune</u>   C42
<u>Books</u>, October 16, p. 6.
    Review of <u>Memoirs of Catherine the Great of Russia</u>,
    translated by Katherine Anthony.

1928

"Misplaced Emphasis." <u>New York Herald Tribune Books</u>,   C43
June 3, p. 7.
    Review of <u>We Are Incredible</u>, by Margery Latimer.

"Magic." <u>transition</u>, XIII (Summer), pp. 229-231.   C44

"Hand-Book of Magic." <u>New Republic</u>, LV (July 25), p. 257.   C45
    Review of <u>A Mirror for Witches</u>, by Esther Forbes.

"Marc Lescarbot." New Republic, LVI (August 22), pp. 24-   C46
25.

> Review of Nova Francise: A Description of Arcadia,
> 1606, translated by P. Erondelle.

"Second Wind." New York Herald Tribune Books, September   C47
23, p. 6.

> A parody review of Useful Knowledge, by Gertrude Stein.

"The Family." New York Herald Tribune Books, October 7,   C48
p. 2.

> Review of Nothing Is Sacred, by Josephine Herbst.

"The Hundredth Role." New York Herald Tribune Books,   C49
October 7, p. 16.

> Review of The Book of Catherine Wells, edited with
> introduction by H.G. Wells.

1929

"The Jilting of Granny Weatherall." transition, XV (Febru-   C50
ary), pp. 139-146.

"The Virgin and the Unicorn." New York Herald Tribune   C51
Books, February 17, pp. 1-2.

> Review of The True Heart, by Sylvia Townsend Warner.

"The Lost Art." New York Herald Tribune Books, March   C52
3, p. 4.

> Review of The Lost Art: Letters of Seven Famous
> Women, edited by Dorothy Van Doren.

"Moral Waxworks Exposed." New York Herald Tribune Books, C53
May 12, p. 4.

> Review of The Devil Is a Woman, by Alice M. Kimball.

"Old Gods and New Messiahs." New York Herald Tribune   C54

<u>Books</u>, September 29, pp. 1-2.

> Review of <u>Idols Behind Altars</u>, by Anita Brenner.

"The Fair-Haired Man." <u>New York Herald Tribune Books</u>,   C55
November 3, p. 1.

> Review of <u>The Gothick North: A Study of Medieval
> Life, Art, and Thought</u>, by Sacheverell Sitwell.

"Theft." <u>The Gyroscope</u>, (November), pp. 21-25.   C56

"Bohemian Futility." <u>New Masses</u>, V (November), pp. 15-16. C57

> Review of <u>Money for Love</u>, by Josephine Herbst.

"The Most Catholic King." <u>New York Herald Tribune Books</u>,   C58
December 1, p. 5.

> Review of <u>King Soldier: Some Aspects of Louis XI
> of France</u>, by D.B. Wyndham Lewis.

"The Frescoes of Diego Rivera." <u>New York Herald Tribune</u>   C59
<u>Books</u>, December 22.

> Review of <u>The Frescoes of Diego Rivera</u>, edited with
> introduction by Ernestine Evans.

1930

"A Disinherited Cosmopolitan." <u>New York Herald Tribune</u>   C60
<u>Books</u>, February 16, p. 22.

> Review of <u>Essays on American Literature</u>, by
> Lafcadio Hearn.

"Flowering Judas." <u>Hound and Horn</u>, III, 2 (Spring),   C61
pp. 316-331.

1931

"Leaving the Petate." <u>New Republic</u> LXV (February 4),   C62
pp. 318-320.

"Example to the Young." New Republic, LXVI (April 22),   C63
pp. 279-280.

> Review of Kay Boyle's Wedding Day and Plagued by
> the Nightingale.

1932

"Bouquet for October" (poem). Pagany, III, 1 (Winter),   C64
pp. 21-22.

"The Cracked Looking-Glass." Scribner's Magazine, XCI   C65
(May), pp. 271-276.

'Hacienda." Virginia Quarterly Review, VIII (October), pp.   C66
556-569.

1934

"A Bright Particular Faith." Hound and Horn, VII, 2 (Spring), C67
pp. 246-257.

'That Tree." Virginia Quarterly Review, X (July), pp. 351-   C68
361.

1935

"Two Plantation Portraits." Virginia Quarterly Review, XI   C69
(January), pp. 85-92.

'The Grave." Virginia Quarterly Review, XI (April), pp.   C70
177-183.

'The Circus." The Southern Review, I, 1 (July), pp. 36-41.   C71

1936

"Rope." Scholastic, XXVIII (March 7), pp. 4-6.   C72

'Noon Wine." Signatures, I (Spring), (pages not numbered).   C73

"The Old Order." The Southern Review, I, 3 (Winter), pp.   C74
495-509.

"History on the Wing." New Republic, LXXXIX (November   C75
8), p. 82.
    Review of The Stones Awake: A Novel of Mexico,
    by Carleton Beals.

1937

"Rivera's Personal Revolution in Mexico." New York Herald   C76
Tribune Books, March 21, p. 7.
    Review of Portrait of Mexico, paintings by Diego
    Rivera and text by Bertram D. Wolfe.

"Dulce Et Decorum Est." New Republic, XC (March 31),   C77
pp. 244-245.
    Review of None Shall Look Back, by Caroline Gordon.

"Noon Wine." Story, X (June), pp. 71-103.   C78

"The Art of Katherine Mansfield." Nation, CXLV (October   C79
23), pp. 435-436.

"The First American Saint." New York Herald Tribune Books, C80
December 12, p. 2.
    Review of The Life of Saint Rose, by Marion Storm.

1938

"Old Mortality." The Southern Review, II (Spring), pp. 686- C81
735.*

"Pale Horse, Pale Rider." The Southern Review, III (Win-   C82
ter), pp. 417-466.

---

* The typescript of this story was given to The University of Texas
Library 17 June 1939.

1939

"Promise Kept." Time, XXX (April 10), p. 75.   C83

"Happy Land." Vogue, XCIV (November 1), pp. 48-49, 110-   C84
111, 113.

"The Downward Path to Wisdom." Harper's Bazaar,   C85
MMDCCXXXI (December), pp. 72-73+

1940

"A Day's Work." Nation, CL (February 10), pp. 205-207.   C86

"A Goat for Azazel" (excerpt from unpublished critical biog-   C87
raphy of Cotton Mather). Partisan Review, VII, 3 (May-
June), pp. 188-199.

"Notes on a Criticism of Thomas Hardy." The Southern   C88
Review, VI (Summer), pp. 150-161.

"Anniversary in a Country Cemetery" (a poem by Miss Por-   C89
ter, music by David Diamond). New York: Independent
Music Publisher. In Harper's Bazaar, MMDCCXLIV (November), p. 139.

1941

"The Source." Accent, I, 3 (Spring), pp. 144-147.   C90

"The Leaning Tower." The Southern Review, VII, 2   C91
(Autumn), pp. 219-279.

"Now at Last a House of My Own." Vogue, XCVIII (Septem-   C92
ber 1), pp. 64-65.

1942

"Lovely, Evocative Photographs." New York Herald Tribune   C93
Books, March 8, p. 4.

Review of New Orleans and Its Living Past, by
D. L. Cohn and John Laughlin.

"Question of Royalties." New York Times, March 8, Sec.   C94
8, p. 10.

"The Sparrow Revolution." Nation, CLIV (March 21), p. 343. C95
Review of The Pink Egg, by Polly Boyden.

"The Charmed Life." Vogue, XCIV (April 15), pp. 45, 97.   C96

"Affectation of Praehiminincies" (excerpt from unpublished   C97
critical biography of Cotton Mather). Accent, II, 3 (Spring),
pp. 131-138; II, 4 (Summer), pp. 226-232.

"No Plot, My Dear, No Story." Writer, LV (June), pp. 167- C98
168.

"American Statement." Mademoiselle, XV (July), pp. 21,   C99
72-73.

1943

"A Song" (translation of a poem by C. Marot). Mademoiselle, C100
XVI (February), p. 180.

"Miss Porter Adds a Comment." Nation, CLVI (March 6),   C101
pp. 358-359.

"Mexico's Thirty Long Years of Revolution." New York   C102
Herald Tribune Books, May 30, pp. 1-2.
Review of The Wind That Swept Mexico, by Anita
Brenner.

"The Winged Skull." Nation, CLVII (July 17), pp. 72-73.   C103
Review of This Is Lorence: A Narrative of the
Reverend Laurence Sterne, by Lodowick Hartley.

"The Days Before." Kenyon Review, V (Autumn), pp. 481- C104
494.

1944
"Portrait: Old South." Mademoiselle, XVIII (February), C105
pp. 89, 151-154.

"Portrait: Old South." Scholastic, XLIV (April 2), pp. 13- C106
14.
    (Permission to reprint granted February 16, 1944,
by Mademoiselle.)

"Kein Haus, Keine Heimat" (story, excerpt from No Safe C107
Harbor). Sewanee Review, LII (October), pp. 465-482.

"China's Plight." The Saratogan, December 15, 1944, p. 6. C108
A letter from Miss Porter and others.

1945
"They Lived with the Enemy in the House." New York C109
Herald Tribune Weekly Book Review, March 4, p. 1.
    Review of Apartment in Athens, by Glenway Wescott.

"The High Sea" (story, excerpt from No Safe Harbor). C110
Partisan Review, XII (Fall), pp. 514-529.

"Pull Dick, Pull Devil." Nation, CLXI (October 13), pp. C111
376-378.
    Review of Saints and Strangers, by G. F. Willison.

1946
"The Strangers." Accent, VI, 4 (Summer), pp. 211-229. C112

"A Christmas Story." Mademoiselle, XXIV (December), pp. C113
155, 277-279. (See A14 and C116. A14 gives a detailed
description of another issue of this item. It was published

by Mademoiselle in 1958 in folder form that simulated a
Christmas card. A staff member of Mademoiselle estimates
that 2500-3000 copies were given to staff members as a
Christmas gift. C116 is a later reprint of this same story
in Scholastic magazine.)

"Embarkation." Sewanee Review, LV (January), pp. 1-23.   C114

"Gertrude Stein: A Self Portrait." Harper's Magazine,   C115
CXCV (December), pp. 519-528.

"A Christmas Story." Scholastic, December.   C116
    (Permission to reprint granted May 19, 1947, by
    Mademoiselle.) (See C113).

"Books I Have Liked." New York Herald Tribune Weekly   C117
Book Review, December 7.

"Love and Hate." Mademoiselle, XXVII (October), pp. 137,   C118
202, 204, 208.

"Books I Have Liked." New York Herald Tribune Weekly   C119
Book Review, December 5.

1949

"The Calm, Pure Art of Willa Cather." New York Times   C120
Book Review, September 25, p. 1.
    Review of Willa Cather on Writing, by Willa Cather.

"The Best Books." New York Times Book Review, p. 4.   C121
    A list, without comment, of ten outstanding books
    of 1949.

"Edith Sitwell's Steady Growth." New York Herald Tribune   C122
Weekly Book Review, December 18, p. 1.
    Review of The Canticle of the Rose, 1917-1949,

by Edith Sitwell.

                                    1950

'Orpheus in Purgatory." New York Times Book Review,   C123
January 1, pp. 3, 10.
      Review of Rilke and Benvenuta, by M. von Hattenberg.

"Measures for Song and Dance" (poem). Harper's Magazine, C124
CC (May), pp. 80-81.

"Pierre-Joseph Redouté." Flair, I (May), pp. 107-108.   C125

"The Flower of Flowers." Flair, I (May), pp. 96-106.   C126

"Virginia Woolf's Essays--a Great Art, a Sober Craft."   C127
New York Times Book Review, May 7, p. 3.
      Review of The Captain's Death Bed and Other Essays,
      by Virginia Woolf.

"This Strange, Old World." New York Times Book Review,   C128
August 20, pp. 5, 17.
      Reviews of The Secret Game, by François Boyer
      (translated from French by Michael Legat), and
      The House of Breath, by William Goyen.

"A Quaker Who Had a Splendid Time of It." New York   C129
Herald Tribune Weekly Book Review, September 24, p. 6.
      Review of Philadelphia Quaker: The Letters of Hanna
      Whitall Smith, edited by Logan Pearsall Smith.

"The Prisoner" (story, excerpt from No Safe Harbor).   C130
Harper's Magazine, CCI (October), pp. 88-96.

"Beerbohm Bailiwick." New York Times Book Review,   C131
October 22, p. 5.
      Review of And Even Now, by Max Beerbohm.

"Yours, Ezra Pound." New York Times Book Review,   C132
October 29, pp. 4, 26.
    Review of The Letters of Ezra Pound, 1907-1941,
    edited by D.D. Paige.

"Under Weigh" (story, excerpt from No Safe Harbor).   C133
Harper's Magazine, CCI (November), pp. 80-88.

"The Future Is Now." Mademoiselle, XXXII (November),   C134
pp. 75, 130-132.

"The Exile" (story, excerpt from No Safe Harbor). Harper's C135
Magazine, CCI (December), pp. 70-78.

1951

"Some Important Authors Speak for Themselves." New York C136
Herald Tribune Book Review, October 12, p. 8.

"Marriage Is Belonging." Mademoiselle, XXXIII (October),   C137
pp. 79, 134-135.

"E.M. Forster Speaks Out for the Things He Holds Dear."   C138
New York Times Book Review, November 4, p. 3.
    Review of Two Cheers for Democracy, by E.M.
    Forster.

"A Most Lively Genius." New York Times Book Review,   C139
November 18, pp. 5, 52.
    Review of The Short Novels of Colette, with an in-
    troduction by Glenway Wescott.

1952

"The Grand and the Tragic." New York Times Book Review, C140
April 13, p. 3.
    Review of Rome and a Villa, by Eleanor Clark.

"Reflections on Willa Cather." <u>Mademoiselle</u>, XXXV (July),   C141
pp. 62-65, 102-104.

1953
"Seducers." <u>Harper's Magazine</u>, CCVII (November), pp.   C142
33-38.

1954
"A Defense of Circe." <u>Mademoiselle</u>, XXXIX (June), pp.   C143
46-48, 96-97.

1955
"Adventure in Living." <u>Mademoiselle</u>, XLI (July), pp. 28-   C144
34.

"November in Windham" (poem). <u>Harper's Magazine</u>, CCXI   C145
(November), p. 44.

1956
"Ship of Fools" (story, excerpt from <u>No Safe Harbor</u>).   C146
<u>Atlantic Monthly</u>, CXCVII, 3 (March), pp. 33-38.

"<u>Noon Wine</u>: the Sources." <u>Yale Review</u>, XLVI, 1   C147
(September), pp. 22-39.

"Gift of Woman." <u>Woman's Home Companion</u>, XXCIII   C148
(December), pp. 29-33+.

1957
"After a Long Journey" (poem). <u>Mademoiselle</u>, XLVI   C149
(November), pp. 142-143.

1958
"Ship of Fools" (story, excerpt from <u>No Safe Harbor</u>).   C150
<u>Mademoiselle</u>, XLVII (July), pp. 26-43.

[A letter from Miss Porter to the students of Edison High   C151
School, Edison, Oklahoma.] Sophomore Vignettes 58-59.
(The original letter is reproduced on the fourth page, un-
numbered.)

1959
"Ship of Fools" (story, excerpt from Ship of Fools). Texas   C152
Quarterly, II, 3 (Autumn), pp. 97-151.

"A Wreath for the Gamekeeper." Shenandoah, XI, 1   C153
(Autumn), pp. 3-12.

1960
"Fig Tree." Harper's Magazine, CCXX (June), pp. 55-59.   C154

"Holiday." Atlantic Monthly, CCVI, 6 (December), pp. 44-   C155
56.

1961
"On First Meeting T.S. Eliot." Shenandoah, XII, 3 (Spring),   C156
pp. 25-26.

1964
"Paris: A Little Incident in the Rue de L'Odeon." Ladies'   C157
Home Journal, XXCI (August), pp. 54-55.

"Violeta." Redbook, CXXIV (December), pp. 36-37.   C158

"Her Legend Will Live." Ladies' Home Journal, LXXXI,   C159
2 (March), pp. 58-59. (A tribute to Jacqueline Kennedy.)

1965
"From the Notebooks of Katherine Anne Porter." The   C160
Southern Review, I (n.s.), 3 (Summer), pp. 570-573.

1966

"Books and Art" [book review section], San Antonio Express/C161
News, January 9, 1966, p. 6-H.
>A letter from Miss Porter to Mr. Gerald Ashford,
>Book Review Editor, in answer to an inquiry he
>wrote to Miss Porter about her exact birthplace
>and early home.

"Katherine Anne Porter Tells Editor About Her Birthplace,"   C162
San Antonio Express/News, March 13, 1966, p. 4-H.
>A letter from Miss Porter to Mr. Gerald Ashford,
>Book Review Editor, giving "new details of her
>childhood in Texas."

"Miss Porter Gets Last Word." San Antonio Express/News,   C163
April 3, 1966, p. 8-H.
>A letter from Miss Porter to Mr. Gerald Ashford,
>Book Review Editor, written to "patch up one more
>little spot in my personal history."

D. TRANSLATIONS

1942   THE ITCHING PARROT   D1

THE ITCHING / PARROT El Periquillo / Sarniento BY JOSÉ
JOAQUÍN FERNÁNDEZ DE / LIZÁRDI (The Mexican Thinker)
Translated from / the Spanish, and with an Introduction by /
KATHERINE ANNE PORTER / [ornament] / GARDEN CITY,
NEW YORK / DOUBLEDAY, DORAN AND CO., INC. 1942
(8 x 5-1/4) (copy examined has been rebound and gatherings are
impossible to determine): pp. 1 blank leaf, xlvi, 292.

Contents: Blank leaf; [i-ii], half title, verso blank; [iii-iv], title,
on verso, imprint, copyright notice, and "FIRST EDITION"; [v-vi],
"Let no one say this is his portrait, but remember there are many
devils who resemble one another. If anyone is stained, let him
cleanse himself as well as he can, for this is more important to
him than criticism and examination of my thought, my locution, my
ideas, and other defects of my work." [signed] TORRES VILLAR-
ROEL, verso blank; vii-viii, acknowledgments; ix-xii, table of contents; xiii-xliv, introduction, verso of last leaf blank; [xlv-xlvi], fly-
title, verso blank; [1]-3, prologue; 4-287, text; 288-292, epilogue,
last leaf blank.

Identification of edition on copyright page: FIRST EDITION.
Published 20 March 1942.

1933   KATHERINE ANNE PORTER'S FRENCH SONG BOOK   D2
KATHERINE / ANNE / PORTER'S / French Song-Book /
HARRISON / OF / PARIS [entire page enclosed with musical
notation]
(11-1/4 x 7-1/2): pp. 78.

Contents: [1-2], blank leaf; [3-4], pre-title page containing author's
name, title of book, one line of music, and a long note by the author, verso blank; [5-6], title, with entire page enclosed in musical
notation, on verso "Printed in Holland"; [7-8], one-page note by the
author, verso blank; 9-78, text, verso of p. 76 and all of last leaf
blank.

Issued in blue boards, quarter bound in ruby-red buckram, spine
titled in gilt.

This book was issued in two variants: one limited to 595 copies, all signed by the author; the other, a de luxe edition of 15 copies, also signed by Miss Porter, on Guarro handmade paper. Copy 499 of the former was the one examined for this entry.

Publisher's Weekly for December 9, 1933, states: "Famous old French songs in the original and with new English rhymed translations. There is a musical example of each melody by Paul Koch and an introduction giving an account of the origin of the song." The seventeen songs comprising the book contain words in both French and English. They range over about a six-hundred-year period.

Published in September 1933; however, the United States copyright office stamp is 19 April 1934, and the English Catalogue of Books gives the publication date as December 1933.

E. BOOKS AND SECTIONS OF BOOKS

Aaron, Daniel. Writers on the Left. New York: Harcourt,   E1
Brace and World, 1961, pp. 170, 236.

Mention of Miss Porter's arrest for participating in a protest
against the Sacco-Vanzetti affair and of her signing a letter to The
New Republic which struck out at Humanism as not helpful to contemporary art.

Aldridge, John W. "Art and Passion in Katherine Anne Por-   E2
ter." In his Time to Murder and Create: The Contemporary
Novel in Crisis. New York: D. McKay, 1966, pp. 178-184.

Miss Porter's lack of intensity, defended by Edmund Wilson
(I104), is seen as limitation. "She has been most careful to take
no imaginative risks that she could not easily and gracefully put into words." Much of this discussion is taken from Aldridge's review of The Collected Stories (I213).

Auchincloss, Louis. "Katherine Anne Porter." In his Pio-   E3
neers and Caretakers: A Study of Nine American Women Novelists.
Minneapolis: University of Minnesota Press, 1965, pp. 136-151.

Biographical sketch and discussion of four of the short stories and Ship of Fools. "Old Mortality" represents Miss Porter's
theme, "the question whether the American past (the Southern Past)
has as much dignity and romance as it appears to have had...."
The theme of "a senseless present" in "Pale Horse, Pale Rider,"
and the theme of "the existence...of an almost ungraspable human
malignity that may well be fated to triumph over life itself" in
"Noon Wine" are discussed. "The Leaning Tower" attempts to "understand the logic of this...failure of man in the Western World."
Ship of Fools "traces this failure to its sources."

Bates, Herbert Ernest. The Modern Short Story. London: E4
Thomas Nelson and Sons, 1941, pp. 14, 180, 185-187.

Miss Porter is seen as "the most accomplished writer, yet
not the most individual writer, of the short story in America today."
"Old Mortality" and "The Old Order" would set Miss Porter down
as a painter of romantic domestic interiors "but 'Noon Wine' shat-

ters the illusion...is as masculine as Hemingway." "Pale Horse,
Pale Rider" is a "recreation of the atmospheric tension of America
in 1918."

Beardsley, Monroe, Robert Daniel, and Glen Leggett. Aids to   E5
Study for Theme and Form: An Introduction to Literature. Englewood Cliffs, N.J.: Prentice-Hall, 1956, pp. 85-86.
    Discussion of "The Grave."

Berkman, Sylvia. Katherine Mansfield. New Haven, Conn: E6
Yale University Press, 1951, pp. 177, 198.
    Miss Porter's critical opinion of Miss Mansfield's art.

Blair, Walter, Theodore Hornberger, James E. Miller, and   E7
Randall Stewart, eds. The Literature of the United States. Chicago: Scott Foresman, 1957, p. 1270.
    Biographical sketch and brief comment. Miss Porter "has
achieved high distinction in the art of short fiction."

Bode, Carl. "Auditor's Report: Prose." In his The Half-   E8
World of American Culture. Carbondale, Ill: Southern Illinois
University Press, 1965, pp. 210-225.
    Reprint of I135.

Bogan, Louise. "Flowering Judas." In her Selected Criti-   E9
cisms: Prose, Poetry. New York: Noonday Press, 1955, pp. 33-
35.
    Reprint of I14.

Bradbury, John. Renaissance in the South: a Critical His-   E10
tory of the Literature 1920-1960. Chapel Hill: University of North
Carolina Press, 1963, pp. 70-74, passim.
    A discussion of Miss Porter's place in the "symbolic na-
turalist tradition." "Her selective scrupulosity in detailing the na-
tural scene and her inconspicuous subtle manipulation of concrete
symbols place her directly in the major Southern pattern." "Flow-

ering Judas, " "Hacienda, " "The Leaning Tower, " "Noon Wine, "
"Old Mortality, " and "Pale Horse, Pale Rider" are discussed.
Miss Porter's role in the Southern Literary Renaissance is men-
tioned throughout the book.

Brooks, Cleanth, and Robert Penn Warren, eds.   The Scope   E11
of Fiction.   New York: Appleton-Century-Crofts, 1960, pp. 227,
326.
     Comment on "Theft" and a biographical sketch.   "Theft" is
"the story of a woman who comes suddenly to a realization...that
she herself is the thief who will leave her nothing. "

--and John T. Purser, eds.   An Approach to Literature.   E12
New York: Appleton-Century-Crofts, 1952, pp. 218-219.
     Comment on "Noon Wine. "   It is "about the difficult defini-
tion of guilt and innocence. "

Burnett, Whit and Hallie Burnett.   The Modern Short Story   E13
in the Making.   New York: Hawthorn Books, 1964, pp. 404-405.
     Discussion of Miss Porter's contribution to the development
of the short novel, a biographical note, and Miss Porter's comments
on the various story forms.

Current-Garcia, Eugene and Walton R. Patrick.   "The Short   E14
Story in America. "   In their ed. American Short Stories.   New
York: Scott, Foresman, 1952, pp. xliii, 1, 462-463; New York:
Scott, Foresman, 1964, pp. 1-li, 423-424.
     Miss Porter is considered a member of an experimental
group, along with "Caldwell, Nelson Algren, ..., William Saroyan
and J.F. Powers. "   Her short stories are "intensely subjective and
often super subtle in effect. "   General comments precede a printing
of "Flowering Judas. "   "Among the special qualities of Miss Porter's writing are her prose style, which has the precision and meta-
phorical richness of poetry; and her use of symbolism which, if
subtle and complex, is yet clear. "   1964 edition adds the comment
that Miss Porter has at last achieved "widespread acclaim (ironical-

118   Katherine Anne Porter

ly on the basis of an inferior work, Ship of Fools) which her con-
summate artistry deserved many years ago."

Ellis, Milton, Louise Pound, George Weida Spohn, and   E15
Frederick J. Hoffman, eds. Revised by F.J. Hoffman. A College
Book of American Literature. New York: American Book Com-
pany, 1956, pp. 1058-1060.
    Discussion of Miss Porter's art, mostly by quotation.
Brief bibliography.

Emmons, Winfred S. KATHERINE ANNE PORTER: THE   E16
REGIONAL STORIES. Austin, Texas: Steck-Vaughn, 1967.
    A study of Miss Porter as a Southern writer whose southern
quality is less intense than Faulkner's or Eudora Welty's. Her
background and her comments on other authors are related to her
own writing. "Flowering Judas," "Hacienda," "The Leaning Tower,"
"The Old Order," and "Noon Wine" are summarized and analyzed
for theme and style.

Gardner, John and Lennis Dunlap, eds. The Forms of Fic-   E17
tion. New York: Random House, 1962, pp. 40-42.
    A brief comment on "The Witness" as a "sketch, not a
story...no real conflict is established," followed by a series of
several questions about character and theme.

Gettmann, Royal A. and Bruce Harkness. A Teacher's Man-   E18
ual for "A Book of Stories." New York: Rinehart, 1955, p. 534.
    A short biographical sketch.

Gilkes, Lillian B. "On Writing the Short Story." In   E19
Dorothy Brewster, ed. A Book of Contemporary Short Stories.
New York: Macmillan Co., 1936, pp. 703-705.
    Discussion of "Mariá Concepción" as an "example of a situa-
tion developed through action" rather than simple delineation of
character.

Gold, Herbert and David L. Stevenson, eds. <u>Stories of</u>   E20
<u>Modern America</u>. New York: St. Martin Press, 1961, pp. 294,
306.

    Biographical note and brief "editor's analysis" of "Flowering
Judas."

Gray, James. <u>On Second Thought</u>. Minneapolis: University   E21
of Minnesota Press, 1946, p. 247.

    Brief note on the scarcity of Miss Porter's achievement.

Greenbaum, Leonard. <u>The Hound and Horn: the History of</u>   E22
<u>a Literary Quarterly</u>. The Hague: Mouton, 1966, pp. 51, 266.

    Mention of Miss Porter's "Flowering Judas" appearing in
the quarterly and a listing of Yvor Winters' review of "Flowering
Judas." (I40, F69).

Hall, James B. and Joseph Langland, eds. <u>The Short Story</u>.   E23
New York: Macmillan, 1956, pp. 381-382.

    A discussion of "Theft" in which the different kinds of
thefts are considered as they relate to the central character. "Each
encounter costs someone something...from these naturalistic de-
tails emerges a statement concerning the nature of life."

Havighurst, Walter. <u>Instructor's Manual for "Masters of the</u>   E24
<u>Modern Short Story."</u> New York: Harcourt, Brace, 1955, p. 24.

    Explication of "The Jilting of Granny Weatherall."

Heilman, Robert B., ed. <u>Modern Short Stories</u>. New York: E25
Harcourt, Brace, 1950, pp. 192-194.

    Discussion of "Flowering Judas." "Here there is much
more than the political; in Laura's experiences there is really
dramatized a very general conflict between the ideal and the actual."

Heiney, Donald. <u>Recent American Literature</u>. Great Neck,   E26
N.Y.: Barron's Educational Series, 1958, pp. 317-323, 587.

    A bibliographical sketch and summaries of the plots of the

chief works.

Hendrick, George. KATHERINE ANNE PORTER. New York: E27
Twayne Publishers, 1965.

    A valuable study of Miss Porter's life, prose fiction and
essays. Following a "Chronology" and a biographical chapter,
Hendrick orders the stories into three sections: the Mexican scene,
fictionalized autobiography, and stories with "Southwestern, univer-
salized, Irish and German settings, attempting at all times to show
Miss Porter's mastery of the short story form." American, English and German criticism of Ship of Fools is surveyed in Chapter
Five; and the sources are carefully examined. The novel is summarized with little critical comment. A chapter is devoted to the
essays. Miss Porter's negligible popular acceptance and high
achievement as an artist are attributed to her honesty.

Hoffman, Frederick John, Charles Allen, and C.F. Ulrich.   E28
The Little Magazine: A History and a Bibliography. Princeton,
N.J.: Princeton University Press, 1946, pp. 135, 208, 285, 291,
325, 336, 350, 392.

    Appearances of Miss Porter's writings are listed in a biblio-
graphical essay on the little magazine.

Jones, Llewelyn. "Contemporary Fiction." In John Albert   E29
Macy, ed. American Writers on American Literature. New York:
Horace Liveright, 1931, p. 502.

    Comment on Miss Porter's achievement in Flowering Judas:
"What Willa Cather has been to the present decade, Miss Porter is
going to be to the next." Her work is also compared to Thornton
Wilder's.

Joselyn, Sister M., O.S.B. "Animal Imagery in Katherine   E30
Anne Porter's Fiction." In Bernice Slote, ed. Myth and Symbol.
Lincoln: University of Nebraska Press, 1963, pp. 101-115.

    An examination of Miss Porter's "consistent use of imagery
relating human beings to animals and animal life" in "Flowering

Judas," "Pale Horse, Pale Rider," "The Leaning Tower," "The Circus," "The Downward Path to Wisdom," and Ship of Fools.

Josephson, Matthew. Life Among the Surrealists. New York: E31 Holt, Rinehart, and Winston, 1962, pp. 352-354.

An account of the author's role in Miss Porter's early career in New York, particularly dealing with the writing of "Flowering Judas."

"Katherine Anne Porter: Pale Horse, Pale Rider." In Allen E32 Angoff, ed. American Writing Today: Its Independence and Vigor. New York: New York University Press, 1957, pp. 399-401.

Reprint of I50.

Kenner, Hugh, ed. Studies in Change: A Book of the Short E33 Story. Englewood Cliffs, N.J.: Prentice-Hall, 1965, pp. xi-xii.

A brief comment on "The Grave." "The whole story resembles a ritual which its participants enact without understanding what it means" but with a realization about the mysteries of life and death.

Ludwig, Richard M. and Marvin B. Berry, eds. Nine Short E34 Novels. Boston: D.C. Heath, 1964, pp. 574-575.

Comments on Miss Porter's stories and her advice to young writers.

Magalaner, Marvin and Edmond L. Volpe. Teacher's Manual E35 to Accompany "Twelve Short Stories." New York: Macmillan, 1961, pp. 14-15.

Explication of "Flowering Judas."

Matthiessen, Francis O. "The Pattern of Literature." In E36 his Changing Patterns in American Civilization. Philadelphia: University of Pennsylvania, 1949, pp. 52-53.

--. "That True and Human World." In Kerker Quinn and E37

Charles Shattuck, eds. Accent Anthology. New York: Harcourt,
Brace, 1946, pp. 619-623.
   Reprint of F113.

Miller, James E., Jr. and Bernice Slote. Notes for Teach-   E38
ing "The Dimensions of the Short Story." New York: Dodd and
Mead, 1967, pp. 28-29.
   A study of "The Grave" with questions for discussion.

Mooney, Harry John, Jr. THE FICTION AND CRITICISM OF   E39
KATHERINE ANNE PORTER. Pittsburgh: University of Pittsburgh
Press, 1957. Revised edition, 1962.
   The first monograph on Miss Porter's work. The Days Before is discussed: Grandmother and Miranda are analyzed as
drawn from the first six short stories in The Leaning Tower. The
novelettes are discussed: "Both 'The Leaning Tower' and 'Hacienda'
deal with political concepts...as their mysterious, destructive
force is felt by the individual." The 1962 edition adds a chapter
on Ship of Fools.

Millett, Fred B. Contemporary American Authors. New   E40
York: Harcourt, Brace, 1940, pp. 96-97, 528, 689.
   Miss Porter is mentioned in a discussion of subjectivity in
the short story. "Although she errs in the direction of super subtlety, her writing has a very rare poetic power, and her suggestiveness, in this form, is almost incomparable." Her works and life
are briefly discussed, and she is listed as a "Short-Story Writer"
under "Authors by Types."

Nance, William L., S.N. KATHERINE ANNE PORTER AND   E41
THE ART OF REJECTION. Chapel Hill: University of North Carolina Press, 1964.
   A detailed study of all of Miss Porter's prose fiction, including Ship of Fools, as it is united by "one central impulse...the
principle of rejection." The author often evaluates Miss Porter as
well as her works, partly because she "made little effort to conceal

the almost complete autobiographical nature of her principal heroine..." (G7).

Norman, Charles. Ezra Pound. New York: Macmillan,   E42
1960, p. 432.
   Miss Porter is listed as one of the judges who voted to
award the first Bollingen Prize for Poetry to Ezra Pound.

Nyren, Dorothy, ed. "Katherine Anne Porter." In her A   E43
Library of Literary Criticism: Modern American Literature. New
York: Frederick Ungar Publishing Co., 1960, pp. 378-380.
   A collection of critical comments about Miss Porter which
appeared in periodicals dating from 1930 to 1952.

O'Brien, Edward J., ed. The Best Short Stories of 1923.   E44
Boston: Small, Maynard, 1923, p. 454.
   Miss Porter "has had a varied and colorful experience in
writing political pamphlets for Mexican revolutionists, essays on
Mexican art, and short stories."

Orvis, Mary B. The Art of Writing Fiction. New York: E45
Prentice-Hall, 1948, pp. 27, 54, 66, 97, 105-107, 123-125, 167.
   Explication of "He," "Rope," "The Downward Path to Wis-
dom," and "Theft."

Peden, William Howard. The American Short Story. Boston: E46
Houghton Mifflin, 1964, p. 17 and passim.
   Mention of Miss Porter as "one of the diverse writers who
found the short story challenging." The sale of Ship of Fools
showed that the public was ready for "something more demanding
than the drivel of big magazines." Miss Porter is "outside the
movement" of literature during the period covered by this book,
having done her major writing prior to 1940.

Rabkin, Leslie. Psychopathology and Literature. San Fran-   E47
cisco: Chandler, 1966, p. 271.

"He" is seen as expressing "conflicting parental attitudes"
of parents of mentally retarded children.

Rideout, Walter B.   Instructor's Manual for "The Experience   E48
of Prose." New York: Crowell, 1960, pp. 17-18.
     Explication of "Flowering Judas."

Rubin, Louis D., Jr.   The Faraway Country: Writers of the   E49
Modern South.   Seattle: University of Washington Press, 1963, pp.
13, 133, 235, 239.
     Miss Porter is discussed as a writer of the South who no
longer lives there but is still producing, having "brought out one of
the most impressive novels of her generation." She is part of "a
literary renascence...."

Ryan, Marjorie. "Katherine Anne Porter: Ship of Fools and   E50
the Short Stories." In Wayne C. Booth, The Rhetoric of Fiction.
Chicago: 1962, pp. 274-277.
     Reprint of F142.

Sale, William, Joseph Hall, and Martin Steinmann.   Critical   E51
Discussions for Teachers Using "Short Stories: Tradition and Direction." Norfolk, Conn: New Directions, 1949, pp. 44-47.
     Explication of "The Old Order."

Satin, Joseph, ed.   Reading Prose Fiction.   Boston: E52
Houghton Mifflin, 1964, pp. 515-516.
     Explication of "Flowering Judas."

--. Reading Literature. Boston: Houghton Mifflin, 1968,   E53
pp. 99-100.
     Reprint of E52.

Schorer, Mark. "Afterword." In Katherine Anne Porter,   E54
Pale Horse, Pale Rider. New York: New American Library, 1962,
pp. 167-175.

Discussion of the three stories in the volume. "Old Mortality," drawn from Miss Porter's past, "is the account of /Miranda's/ long effort to detach herself from the beguilements of the legend" of the past. "Noon Wine" is about a world not as "deceptively romantic," a world of "the sudden horror of the present." Miranda of "Pale Horse, Pale Rider" is Miss Porter, the artist who must know the past, present and future.

Shirer, William. Mid Century Journey. New York: Farrar, E55
Straus and Young, 1952, pp. 1-2.
  Miss Porter is described as "another and older and also very discerning writer...reflecting on the threatening times."

Short, Raymond and Richard B. Sewall. A Manual for Teach- E56
ers Using "Short Stories for Study." Revised edition. New York:
Holt, 1950, pp. 51-54.
  A study of "Pale Horse, Pale Rider."

Simonson, Harold P. Instructor's Manual to Accompany E57
"Trio: A Book of Stories, Plays and Poems." New York: Harper
and Row, 1965, pp. 9-10.
  Explication of "Flowering Judas."

Singleton, Ralph H. Instructor's Manual for "Two and E58*
Twenty: A Collection of Short Stories." New York: St. Martin's
Press, 1962, pp. 14-15.

Six Great Modern Short Novels. New York: Dell, 1954, E59
p. 155.
  Biographical sketch and mention of Miss Porter's works.

Sklare, Arnold B. The Art of the Novella. New York: Mac- E60
millan, 1965, pp. 297-298.
  Comment on "Pale Horse, Pale Rider."

Snell, George Dixon. "A Forecast." In his The Shapers of E61

American Fiction. New York: E.P. Dutton and Co., 1947, p. 301.
        Elements of Hawthorne and Henry James are seen in some
of the stories.

Stallman, Robert W. "Life, Art and 'the Secret Sharer'."   E62
In William Van O'Connor, ed. Forms of Modern Fiction. Minneapolis: University of Minnesota Press, 1948, pp. 230-231.
        A discussion of Miss Porter's methods of writing, quoting
from her journals.

Stegner, Wallace and Mary Stegner, eds. Great American   E63
Short Stories. New York: Dell, 1957, p. 27.
        Brief discussion of Miss Porter's "pure, slim productions."

Steinmann, Martin and Gerald Willen, eds. Literature for   E64
Writing. Belmont, Calif: Wadsworth, 1962, pp. 183-184.
        Study of "Flowering Judas."

--. Great American Short Stories. Second Edition. New   E65
York: Dell, 1967, pp. 176-177.
        Reprint of E64.

Straumann, Heinrich. American Literature in the Twentieth   E66
Century. London: Hutchinson House, 1951, pp. 91-93, 126.
        Miss Porter and Glenway Wescott are seen as "representa-
tives of...the genteel tradition of psychological fiction."

Summers, Richard. The Craft of the Short Story. New York: E67
Rinehart and Company, 1948, pp. 283-285.
        Study of "Flowering Judas" and a biographical sketch which
is partly an interview with Miss Porter about her writing.

Thompson, Barbara. "Katherine Anne Porter: An Interview." E68
In Writers at Work. Second Series. New York: Viking, 1963,
pp. 137-164.
        Reprint of F159.

Van Gelder, Robert. "Katherine Anne Porter at Work."   E69
In his Writers and Writing. New York: Charles Scribner's Sons,
1946, pp. 42-44.
    Reprint of F162.

Walker, Warren S. Twentieth-Century Short Story Explication. E70
Hamden, Conn: The Shoe String Press, 1961, pp. 312-319.
Checklist of explications of the short stories.

--. Twentieth-Century Short Story Explication: Supplement.   E71
Hamden, Conn: The Shoe String Press, 1963, pp. 103-106.
Further listings of explications of the short stories.

--. Twentieth-Century Short Story Explication: Supplement II. E72
Hamden, Conn: The Shoe String Press, 1965, pp. 133-139.
Further listings of explications.

Wanning, Andrews. "The Literary Situation in America."   E73
In Balachandra Rajan, ed. The Novelist as Thinker. London:
Dobson, Ltd., 1947, pp. 154-166 /156-157/.
    Miss Porter is compared to Eudora Welty and Carson Mc-
Cullers. William Faulkner and Miss Porter "appear to continue as
the divergent models for the younger writers."

Warren, Robert Penn. "Irony with a Center: Katherine Anne E74
Porter." In his Selected Essays. New York: Random House,
1958, pp. 136-156.
    Reprint of F170.

--. "Irony with a Center: Katherine Anne Porter." In   E75
Robert E. Knoll, ed. Contrasts. Second edition. New York:
Harcourt, Brace, 1951, pp. 492-502.
    Reprint of F170.

--. "Irony with a Center: Katherine Anne Porter." In   E76
Herbert Gold and David L. Stevenson, eds. Stories of Modern

America. New York: St. Martin's Press, 1961, pp. 459-474.
Reprint of F170.

Weber, Brom, ed. The Letters of Hart Crane. New York: E77
Hermitage House, 1952, pp. 364, 369-370, 373, 375, 377-378, 383.
Letters written during the period from April 30, 1931 to
October 5, 1931 to Miss Porter and others concerning their friend-
ship and their quarrel, and the effect of that quarrel on their lives.

Welker, Robert L. and Herschel Gower. The Sense of Fic-   E78
tion. Englewood Cliffs, N.J.: Prentice-Hall, 1966, pp. 150-154.
A study of "The Grave."

Wescott, Glenway. "Katherine Anne Porter." In Clarence   E79
Wachner, Frank E. Ross, and Eva Marie Houten, eds. Contemporary American Prose. New York: Macmillan, 1963, pp. 282-
287.
Reprint of I207.

--. "Katherine Anne Porter Personally." In his Images of   E80
Truth: Remembrances and Criticism. New York: Harper and
Row, 1962, pp. 25-58.
Personal observations made from experiences shared by the
author and Miss Porter and how these experiences reflect themes
in the short stories. "Pale Horse, Pale Rider," "Old Mortality,"
"The Grave," and "Noon Wine" are discussed. The history of the
writing of Ship of Fools is also discussed. (F173, I207).

West, Ray B. "'Flowering Judas'." In Robert Stallman and   E81
Arthur Waldhorn, eds. American Literature, Readings and Critique.
New York: G.P. Putnam, 1961, pp. 767-770.
Originally appeared as 'Katherine Anne Porter: Symbol and
Theme in 'Flowering Judas'." See F175.

--. KATHERINE ANNE PORTER. Minneapolis: University   E82
of Minnesota Press, 1963.

University of Minnesota Pamphlet on American Writers, No.
28. "As a non-practicing Catholic and a liberal Southerner, Miss
Porter has found the principal themes in her fiction in the tensions
provided between fixed social and moral positions and the necessi-
ties of movement and alteration." These themes are discussed as
they appear in the stories which utilize Miss Porter's background,
shaped into a mythical legend of a past. Ship of Fools, differing
"in the necessary richness of the longer work in the technical excellence that integrates and unifies so diverse a body of material,"
and its criticism are discussed.

--. "Katherine Anne Porter and Historic Memory." In   E83
Louis D. Rubin and Robert D. Jacobs, eds. Southern Renaissance:
The Literature of the Modern South. Baltimore: John Hopkins
Press, 1953, pp. 278-289.
    Reprint of F174.

--. "Katherine Anne Porter and Historic Memory." In   E84
Louis D. Rubin and Robert D. Jacobs, eds. South: Modern
Southern Literature in Its Cultural Setting. Garden City, N.Y:
Doubleday, 1961, pp. 301-313.
    Reprint of F174.

--. The Short Story in America, 1900-1950. Chicago: E85
Henry Regnery Co., 1952, pp. 72-76.
    Discussion of Miss Porter as a Southern writer. Her use
of her background as a source, her 'Mexican experiences,' and her
early Catholicism are considered. "Flowering Judas," "Pale
Horse, Pale Rider," and "Old Mortality" are discussed as being
her "three most popular stories."

--. "Katherine Anne Porter: Symbol and Theme in 'Flower- E86
ing Judas'." In John Aldridge, ed. Critiques and Essays on Modern Fiction: 1920-1951. New York: Ronald Press, 1952, pp. 217-
230.
    Reprint of F175.

--. "Katherine Anne Porter: Symbol and Theme in 'Flower-   E87
ing Judas'." In Ray B. West and Robert W. Stallman, eds. The
Art of Modern Fiction. New York: Rinehart and Co., 1949, pp.
287-292.
    Reprint of F175.

Whicher, George. In Arthur H. Quinn, ed. The Literature   E88
of the American People. New York: Appleton-Century-Crofts,
1951, p. 925.
    Discussion of Miss Porter in twentieth-century literature.
She "has specialized in the evocation of exotic atmospheres."
"Flowering Judas," "Hacienda," "Pale Horse, Pale Rider," "Noon
Wine" and "The Leaning Tower" are mentioned.

Whitham, Tasker. Panorama of American Literature.   E89
Stephen Daye Press, 1947, pp. 311-314.
    Miss Porter is considered a writer "with none of the tricks
of style which characterize so many contemporary writers" in a
chapter entitled "Realism and Experiment (1920-   )."

Wilson, Edmund. "Katherine Anne Porter." In his Classics   E90
and Commercials. New York: Farrar, Straus, 1950, pp. 219-223.
    Reprint of I104.

Wykes, Alan. A Concise Survey of American Literature.   E91
London: Arthur Barker, 1955, p. 175.
    Miss Porter is considered as a Southern writer who concerns
herself with psychological detail "in preference to essentials" and
thus gains in atmosphere "at the expense of strength." She is compared to Carson McCullers, Eudora Welty and Erskine Caldwell.

F. ARTICLES IN PERIODICALS AND NEWSPAPERS

Aldington, Richard. "A Wreath for Lawrence?" Encounter,   F1
XIV (April, 1960), pp. 51-54.

Comments on Miss Porter's criticism of D.H. Lawrence
(Encounter, February, 1960, pp. 69-77) and defense of Lawrence,
Miss Porter notes recent scholarship and publications about his
life and letters.

Alexander, Jean. "Katherine Anne Porter's Ship in the   F2
Jungle, " Twentieth Century Literature, II (January, 1966), pp.
179-188.

A study of "Pale Horse, Pale Rider" as a preview of the
negative view of the world which Miss Porter's readers seem dis-
mayed to find in Ship of Fools.

Allen, Charles. "Southwestern Chronicle: Katherine Anne   F3
Porter. " Arizona Quarterly, II (Summer, 1946), pp. 90-95.

A discussion of the short stories and novellas which have a
Southwestern or Mexican background. "'María Concepción,' 'Flowering Judas,' 'Hacienda,' and 'Noon Wine'--rank with the best of
her work. " "Flowering Judas" and 'Noon Wine" are discussed as
they "illustrate the two methods of fictional approach which dom-
inate" her three volumes of short stories.

--. "Katherine Anne Porter: Psychology as Art. " Southwest F4
Review, XLI (Summer, 1956), pp. 223-230.

A psychological examination of "The Cracked Looking-Glass. "

--. "The Nouvellas of Katherine Anne Porter. " University   F5
of Kansas City Review, XXIX (December 1962), pp. 87-93.

Discussion of the four short novels: 'Noon Wine"--"a statement about guilt and responsibility"; 'Old Mortality"--an example
of "Miss Porter's ability to project the atmosphere of a particular
social milieu"; "Pale Horse, Pale Rider"--a view of internal evil;
and 'The Leaning Tower"--"the least satisfying" in its pessimistic
description of German character.

Amory, Cleveland. "Celebrity Register." McCall's, XC   F6
(April 1963), p. 184.

Interview with Miss Porter in which she comments about the
reception of Ship of Fools.

"Annual Dinner." Bulletin of the Society for the Libraries of   F7
New York University, May 1940, p. 1.

Announcement of the awarding of the first gold medal of the
society "for literary achievement" to Miss Porter.

Ashford, Gerald. "Books and Art." San Antonio Express and   F8
News, January 9, 1966, p. H-6.

Commenting on a letter from Miss Porter in which she said
"I was born on Indian Creek in Brown County, " the author says,
"Miss Porter fails to mention, and perhaps does not know, that
there is a TOWN called Indian Creek near Brownwood. " He wonders
"why she was so little impressed with San Antonio, at an impres-
sionable age, ... "

--. "Katherine Anne Porter Tells Editor About Her Birth-   F9
place." San Antonio Express and News, March 13, 1966, p. H-4.

Commenting on a letter from Miss Porter about her birthplace, the author wonders "why her childhood home failed to make
a mark on her memory. "

"Author Receives Medal from Library Group." New York   F10
Times, April 4, 1940, p. 24.

The first gold medal of the society (F7) was presented to
Miss Porter by Pearl Buck.

"Author to Lecture on 'Pale Horse'." Baltimore Evening Sun,   F11
October 17, 1956, p. 35.

Announcement of lecture at Goucher College.

"Authors Honored by National Institute." New York Times,   F12
January 18, 1950, p. 23.

"Katherine Anne Porter and Glenway Wescott, writers, were elected vice-presidents of the National Institute of Arts and Letters...."

Baker, Howard. "The Contemporary Short Story." Southern   F13
Review, III (1938), pp. 595-596.

Consideration of Miss Porter as "one of the most 'socially conscious' of our writers." "He" attains "the perfection of a highly selective realistic method; 'Old Mortality" "contains the living stuff out of which our world, or at least part of it, has just emerged"; "'Noon Wine'...invites the analytical eye, for it is classical in its structure. "

--. "The Upward Path: Notes on the Work of Katherine   F14
Anne Porter. " Southern Review, New Series, IV (Winter 1968),
pp. 1-19.

Discussion of Miss Porter as a "modern, a beneficiary of a discipline which has been known as Modernism.... She is akin to Ezra Pound and Pablo Picasso." Joyce's influence is seen in "The Downward Path to Wisdom. " Ezra Pound's influence on Miss Porter and Hart Crane is discussed; the effect of her years in Mexico is seen in "María Concepción. " "Hacienda" and "Flowering Judas" are briefly considered; a large section considers "Noon Wine. " Ship of Fools is discussed.

Becker, Laurence A. "'The Jilting of Granny Weatherall':   F15
The Discovery of Pattern. " English Journal, LV (December 1966),
pp. 1164-1169.

An analysis of the complex pattern of the story which considers two jiltings, first by George and later by God.

Bell, Vereen M. "'The Grave' Revisited. " Studies in Short   F16*
Fiction, III (No. 1, Fall 1965), pp. 39-45.

Berg, Paul. "Celebrating a Celebrated Author. " St. Louis   F17
Post-Dispatch Pictures, April 22, 1962, pp. 4-5.

Criticism--Articles

135

Photograph of Miss Porter, Cleanth Brooks, Miss Irita Van Doren and Bruce Lloyd Wescott and his wife, to whom Miss Porter dedicated her novel; a biographical sketch and comment on her total literary achievement, including Ship of Fools.

"Best Years." Newsweek, LVIII (July 31, 1961), p. 78. F18

An interview with Miss Porter about the writing of Ship of Fools.

"Biographical Sketches of the 1966 Winners of the Pulitzer F19 Prizes." New York Times, May 3, 1966, p. 43.

Birss, John. "American First Editions." Publisher's Weekly, F20 CXXXIII (June 18, 1938), p. 2383.

Listing of first appearances beginning with "Outline of Mexican Popular Arts and Crafts," 1922, and books which published first appearances of short stories.

Bluefarb, Sam. "Loss of Innocence in 'Flowering Judas'." F21 College Language Association Journal, VII (March 1964), pp. 256-262.

A discussion of the initiation motif in "Flowering Judas" as shown in the loss of innocence.

Bode, Winston. "Miss Porter on Writers and Writing." F22 Texas Observer, October 31, 1958, pp. 6-7.

"Book Awards Go to 4 U.S. Writers." New York Times, F23 March 16, 1966, p. 42.

Miss Porter is a recipient of the National Book Award.

"Book Drive Begun." New York Times, January 24, 1960, F24 p. 75.

Miss Porter is a member of the Freedom House Bookshelf Committee.

"Book-of-the-Month Club Awards." Publisher's Weekly,   F25
CXXXI (February 6, 1937), pp. 736-737.

    Announcement of the awarding of four fellowships of $2500
each to Robinson Jeffers, Katherine Anne Porter, James T. Farrell and Paul Sears. Miss Porter received the award for the "pre-
cise and delicate art of her short stories" in Flowering Judas.

"Book Notes." New York Herald Tribune, December 22,   F26
1936, p. 21.

    Announcement of the forthcoming publication of Noon Wine by
Schuman's of Detroit, with comments by Glenway Wescott, Josephine Herbst and Kay Boyle.

Boutell, Clip. "Authors Are Like People." New York Post,   F27
September 21, 1944, p. 23.

    An interview following the publication of The Leaning Tower
and Other Stories.

Boyle, Kay. "Full Length Portrait." New Republic, CV   F28
(November 1941), p. 707.

    A discussion of Miss Porter's introduction to Eudora Welty's
A Curtain of Green /New York: Doubleday, Doran and Co./.

Bride, Sister M. "Laura and the Unlit Lamp." Studies in   F29
Short Fiction, I (Fall 1963), pp. 61-63.

    A discussion of "Flowering Judas" as a condemnation of
"spiritual deadness" rather than of chastity.

"Brilliant Story Was Written in Inn Here." Doylestown,   F30
Pennsylvania Daily Intelligencer, April 15, 1940, pp. 1-2.

    Quotes an interview by Robert Van Gelder (F172) in which
Miss Porter says she wrote a story included in Pale Horse, Pale
Rider in an Inn called the Fountain House, in Doylestown. (F67).

Brooks, Cleanth. "On 'The Grave'." Yale Review, LV   F31
(Fall 1965), pp. 274-279.

Discussion of the story as one "about growing up and going through a kind of initiation into the mysteries of adult life."

Cassini, Igor. "The New 400." Esquire, XXXIX (June 1953), F32
p. 48.
Miss Porter is one of the "New 400" who are "the aristocracy of achievement in this country."

Chamberlain, John. "Books of the Times." New York Times, F33
October 20, 1933, p. 17.
An article about Ford Maddox Ford which mentions his "championing the work of Katherine Anne Porter, whose 'Flowering Judas'...is one of the best books of short stories ever written by an American."

Cowley, Malcolm. "Twenty-five Years After: The Lost Gen- F34
eration Today." Saturday Review of Literature, XXIV (June 2,
1951), p. 7.
Brief biographical note.

Cowser, Robert G. "Porter's 'The Jilting of Granny Weather- F35
all'." Explicator, XXI (December 1962), Item 34.
Brief explication which considers the second jilting, "the one around which the theme revolves."

Cruttwell, Patrick. "Swift, Miss Porter, and the 'Dialect of   F36
the Tribe'." Shenandoah, XVII (Summer 1966), pp. 27-38 /37-38/.
Compares Miss Porter's criticism of "Certain trends and writers in America today" with Swift's criticism of corruption of the English language.

Culligan, Glendy. Bookweek, January 19, 1964, p. 2.   F37
Mrs. Johnson, wife of the President, wished to get in touch with Miss Porter, who had sailed for Rome, to invite her to tea along with other writers.

Cunningham, J.V.   "The 'Gyroscope' Group. "   Bookman,   F38
LXXV (November 1932), pp. 703-708 / 703/.

   Mention of Miss Porter as a contributor to the Gyroscope.

Curley, Daniel.   "Katherine Anne Porter: The Larger Plan. " F39
Kenyon Review, XXV (Autumn 1963), pp. 671-695.

   An article in which the author wishes "to show what her real
virtues are and what her limitations are, and how uncritical acceptance in the United States led her to attempt what was most opposite
her real abilities. " In Ship of Fools, which he calls a "bad book, "
Miss Porter succeeds when she "treats a human being simply as a
human being but when she tries to work in a broader context the
effect is always narrower. " Mr. Curley sees the female protagon-
ists based on Miss Porter's own experiences as successful, but
sees her abandonment of "her personal legend and seeking of a new
fable in a new world" as a limitation.

--.   "Treasure in 'The Grave'. "   Modern Fiction Studies, IX   F40
(Winter 1963-1964), pp. 377-384.

   A study of structure and technique in "The Grave. "

"Dando Calls 'Ship of Fools' Tapestry of Death Dance. "   F41
Hartford, Conn. Times, May 2, 1962, p. 40.

   Report of "a book review talk" by John Dando, "Trinity College assistant professor of English. " Ship of Fools is compared to
Youngblood Hawke.

Deasy, Brother Paul Francis.   "Reality and Escape. "   Four   F42
Quarters, XII (January 1963), pp. 28-31.

   A study of "He" as it illustrates "a preoccupation in all her
work, " a tracing to the source and understanding the logic of what
Miss Porter calls "the majestic and terrible failure of the life of
man in the Western World. "

"Dedicated Author: Katherine Anne Porter. " New York   F43
Times, March 16, 1966, p. 42.

A biographical sketch of Miss Porter on the occasion of the National Book Award.

Denham, Alice. "Katherine Anne Porter, Washington's Own   F44 Literary Lioness." The Washingtonian, I (May 1965), pp. 33, 38-39.

An interview in which Miss Porter's home is described, a biographical sketch appears, and brief comments on her literary production are made.

De Vries, Peter. "Nobody's Fool (A Character or Two Over- F45 looked in Miss Katherine Anne Porter's Shipload)." New Yorker, XXXVIII (June 16, 1962), pp. 28-29.

A satire about Miss Porter and the lengthy preparation of Ship of Fools.

"Dinner Salutes Pulitzer Prizes: Present and Past Winners   F46 Mark 50th Anniversary." New York Times, May 11, 1966, p. 33.

A list of the winners and past winners attending the dinner on the occasion of the Annual Awards presentation.

Dolbier, Maurice. "I've had a Good Run for My Money: An   F47 Interview with Katherine Anne Porter." New York Herald Tribune Book Review, April 1, 1962, pp. 3, 11.

An interview in which Miss Porter discusses the writing of Ship of Fools, the O. Henry Award for a short story (received for "Holiday"), and her opinions of some contemporary writers.

Duff, Charles. Nation, CLV (March 6, 1943), p. 358.   F48

A letter to the editor which comments on a review of The Itching Parrot (172).

Dutourd, Jean. "Homage to the Bed." Harper's Bazaar,   F49 XCVI (June 1962), p. 45.

Portrait of Miss Porter in her bed and a brief mention of Ship of Fools which was "hailed this spring in terms reserved for masterpieces. "

Ehrenpreis, Irwin. "Readable Americans." Revue Des   F50**
Langues Vivantes, XXIV (1, 1968), pp. 416-419.

"Endless Relations: Henry James and Katherine Anne Por-   F51**
ter. " St. Michael's College Alumni News Bulletin, (Spring 1962),
pp. 14-15.

"First Novel." Time, LXXXVIII (July 29, 1961), p. 70.   F52
    A pre-publication interview about the forthcoming Ship of
Fools and its history.

Flood, Ethelbert. "Christian Language in Modern Literature." F53
Culture, XXII (March 1961), pp. 28-42.
    A study of the pattern of Christian details in "Flowering
Judas. " Works of Graham Greene and Thomas Mann are also
studied in this article.

Foley, Eileen. "Katherine Anne Porter Gets a Gift, Day of   F54
Her Own at LaSalle College." Philadelphia Evening Bulletin, October 27, 1961, p. 19.
    An interview on writing and the teaching of writing.

"Ford Fund Gives Writers $105,000." New York Times,   F55
February 16, 1951, p. 31.
    Announcement of the presentation of the first grants from
the Ford Foundation to eleven American novelists and poets, including Miss Porter.

"Four Authors are Given National Book Awards." Publisher's F56
Weekly, CLXXXIX (March 21, 1966), pp. 47-48.
    Announcement of the Award to Miss Porter for her Collected
Stories.

Frankel, Haskel. "Interview with Katherine Anne Porter. "   F57

Saturday Review, XLVIII (September 25, 1965), p. 36.

About her life in the suburbs of Washington, D.C., and descriptions of her appearance and her home.

Fuermann, George. "Post Card." Houston Post, October 6,   F58
1952, Section 2, p. 6.

Note about Mrs. Gay Holloway to whom Miss Porter dedicated The Days Before.

"4 'Forgotten' Books Win $2500 Prize." New York Times,   F59
January 30, 1937, p. 15.

Announcement of the Book-of-the-Month Club award (F25).

"Fund Awards to 77 Aid Creative Work." New York Times,   F60
March 30, 1931, p. 12.

Miss Porter is awarded a Guggenheim Fellowship.

Gannett, Lewis. "Books and Things." New York Herald   F61
Tribune, January 30, 1937, p. 11.

Comments on Miss Porter's Book-of-the-Month Club Award
(F25).

--. "Books and Things." New York Herald Tribune, July   F62
28, 1942, p. 15.

Mention of Miss Porter's "elusive introduction" to Fiesta in
November.

Gardiner, Harold C., ed. "State of the Question, Katherine   F63
Anne Porter." America, CVII (May 26, 1962), pp. 309-312.

Letters to the editor in response to Fr. Gardiner's review
(I152) and his final comment. He feels that he and Dr. Murphy
disagree on the dimness of Miss Porter's view of human nature.
Dubus' objection is a matter of semantics; a critic's job is to question the vision of a writer.

Dubus, André J. "A Letter to the Editor." America,

CVII (May 26, 1962), pp. 311-312.

A criticism of Fr. Gardiner's statement that Ship of Fools is not a novel and that it lacks "positive visions" (I152).

Murphy, Edward F. "A Letter to the Editor." America, CVII (May 23, 1962), pp. 309-311.

A criticism of Fr. Gardiner's analysis of Ship of Fools (I152).

"Girls Give Literature New Third Dimension." New York   F64
Herald Tribune, December 1, 1952, p. 12.

News article about the methods of the girls who recorded Miss Porter's readings.

Girson, Rochelle. "The Author." Saturday Review, XLV   F65
(March 31, 1962), pp. 15-16.

Interview about the publication of Ship of Fools.

Gore, George. "The Best Residuum of Truth." Georgia Re-   F66
view, XX (Fall 1966), pp. 278-291.

Discussion of The Collected Stories. "Holiday" is analyzed at length. It is 'neither propaganda art nor idyll. It is a realistic depiction of what Louise Cowan has called 'the communal world'." Ship of Fools is described as being critized 'largely because it depicts truths which most readers do not yet want to admit." Four book-length studies of Miss Porter's writing are discussed (E27, E39, E41, and E82).

"Great and Near-Great Will Keep 'em Guessing." Doylestown, F67
Pennsylvania Daily Intelligencer, April 16, 1940.

The proprietor of The Water Wheel argues that Miss Porter wrote Pale Horse, Pale Rider at his Inn (F30).

Green, George. "Brimstone and Roses: Notes on Katherine   F68
Anne Porter." Thought, XXXVI (Autumn 1961), pp. 421-440.

A consideration of Miss Porter's unique position in American

Criticism--Articles

letters. Not to be considered with Hemingway, Faulkner, Wilder, Fitzgerald and Marquand, "she has worked hard to free her work from the comfortable repetitions" young writers fall into. Her themes vary, as do her settings. "Hacienda" is discussed at length, the other stories briefly mentioned. Miss Porter's unobtrusive style is stressed.

Greenbaum, Leonard. "The Hound and Horn Archive." Yale   F69
University Library Gazette, XXXIX (January 1965), pp. 137-146
/138/.
        Miss Porter is one of the contributors to the magazine
(E22).

Hafley, James. "'María Concepción': Life Among the Ruins." F70
Four Quarters, XII (November 1962), pp. 11-17.
        Discussion of "María Concepción" in the Katherine Anne Por-
ter Issue which treats the story as "an excellent example of how
meaning in fiction is often most closely related not to plot or to
objects but to achieved verbal form; what language makes as it
realizes substance."

Hagopian, John V. "Katherine Anne Porter: Feeling, Form   F71
and Truth." Four Quarters, XII (November 1962), pp. 1-10.
        A detailed discussion of Miss Porter's writing. Symbolism
in "Old Mortality," "Pale Horse, Pale Rider," and "Flowering
Judas" is discussed. "The Jilting of Granny Weatherall" and "Holiday" are discussed.

Hartley, Lodwick. "Dark Voyagers, A Study of Katherine   F72
Anne Porter's Ship of Fools." University of Kansas City Review,
XXX (December 1963), pp. 83-94.
        A history of the genesis and growth of Ship of Fools, com-
paring it to Brant's Das Narrenschiff. Freudian elements in the
novel are discussed. Treatment of German character in "The Leaning Tower" is compared to its treatment in the novel.

--. "Katherine Anne Porter." Sewanee Review, XLVII   F73
(April 1940), pp. 206-216.

Study of the stories in Flowering Judas and Pale Horse,
Pale Rider. The short stories in Flowering Judas evoke "the feel-
ing that they are embryonic novels." "Noon Wine" is compared to
Steinbeck's Of Mice and Men. "Old Mortality" and "Pale Horse,
Pale Rider" are considered unsuccessful.

--. "The Lady and the Temple: The Critical Theories of   F74
Katherine Anne Porter." College English, XIV (April 1953), pp.
386-391.

A study of the essays in The Days Before as they illustrate
Miss Porter's critical theories. "She wishes to be a classicist in
the Greek tradition both in her practice and her tradition." Although she tries to understand the failure of Western man, she
seems to escape from the central problem. She has taken refuge
from disillusionment "in the temple of art itself."

Heilman, Robert B. "Ship of Fools: Notes on Style." Four   F75
Quarters, XII (November 1962), pp. 46-55.

A discussion of the lack of obvious style in Ship of Fools.
"Miss Porter is an absentee presence: in one sense her style is
no-style...some uninterchangeable (though not unborrowable) advice
that firmly announces 'Faulkner' or 'Hemingway'."

--. "The Southern Temper." Hopkins Review, VI (Fall   F76
1952), pp. 5-15 /5, 9, 11/.

Miss Porter is included in a discussion of Southern writers
who share a "combination of qualities" that make them distinctive.

"A Hemingway First Reading." Boston Sunday Globe, April   F77
29, 1962, pp. 1, 48.

Miss Porter is among guests at a first reading of "an unpublished work by the late author" at the Kennedys' White House
honoring of prize-winners.

Hendrick, George. "Hart Crane Aboard the Ship of Fools: F78
Some Speculations." Twentieth Century Literature, IX (April 1963),
pp. 3-9.

A discussion of Miss Porter's relationship with Crane in
Mexico in 1931 and how it became a part of her novel.

--. "Katherine Anne Porter's 'Hacienda'." Four Quarters,   F79
XII (November 1962), pp. 24-29.

A discussion of the sources of the story. Miss Porter
witnessed the filming of a movie in Mexico and transmuted the experience into fiction. Mr. Hendrick calls the story a "brilliantly
executed...short novel of the lost generation."

Herbst, Josephine. "Miss Porter and Miss Stein." Partisan   F80
Review, XV (May 1948), pp. 568-572.

A comparison of points of view of Picasso, who painted a
portrait of Miss Stein in 1905, and of Miss Porter, who wrote an
article about Miss Stein (Harper's Magazine, December 1947).

Hertz, Robert Neil. "Sebastian Brandt and Porter's Ship of   F81
Fools." Midwest Quarterly, VI (Summer 1964), pp. 389-401.

Discussion of the novel as an allegory. "Miss Porter bor-
rows the idea and inspiration of Brandt without incorporating his
technique and purpose." Her search for the discovery about the
human situation prevails in the short stories and in the novel.

Hoffman, Frederick J. "Katherine Anne Porter's 'Noon Wine'." F82
CEA Critic, XVIII (November 1956), pp. 1, 6-7.

Analysis of "Noon Wine" for the teaching of literature.
"Superficially it is a tragedy of the failure of self-awareness. This
failure becomes the delusion of murder and suicide. The murder
is an act of self-defense with the self not known; the suicide is an
act of violent supererogation." Miss Porter has "made us see that
tragedy is at times after all a consequence of the ways in which
circumstances limit our acts."

Holdridge, Barbara. "Dylan as He Was." New York Herald   F83
Tribune Magazine, January 12, 1964, p. 31.

    Mention of Miss Porter. "Nothing of the spirit of those
days remains now. We are all changed and scattered...Katherine
Anne Porter to popular fame and Washington."

"Individualism for Writers Stressed at Women's Club." New   F84
York Herald Tribune (Paris), November 30, 1935, p. 2.

    Miss Porter gave advice to young writers in a speech "dur-
ing the Book Hour at the American Women's Club."

Janeway, Elizabeth. "Interview with Katherine Anne Porter."   F85
New York Times Book Review, April 1, 1962, pp. 4-5.

    An interview about Miss Porter's career as a writer. She
did not choose to write but now it is the most important thing in
her life.

Johnson, James. "The Adolescent Hero: A Trend in Modern   F86
Fiction." Twentieth Century Literature, V (April 1959), pp. 3-11
/6/.

    "Pale Horse, Pale Rider" is discussed. Miranda is con-
sidered an adolescent heroine.

Johnson, James William. "Another Look at Katherine Anne   F87
Porter." Virginia Quarterly Review, XXXVI (Autumn 1960), pp.
598-613.

    A critical study of Miss Porter's writing and influence. Mr.
Mooney's work (E39) is criticized because he "reads Miss Porter's
fiction within an historical perspective which limits and distorts it."
Mr. Johnson divides the fiction into six units: "the individual within his heritage," "cultural displacement," "unhappy marriage,"
"death of love," "man's slavery to his own nature which dooms him
to suffering and disappointment," and "an amalgam of all Miss Porter's themes."

Johnson, Shirley E. "Love Attitudes in the Fiction of Kather-   F88

ine Anne Porter." <u>West Virginia University Philological Papers</u>,
XII (December 1961), pp. 82-93.

A study of the special characteristics of Miss Porter as a woman writer.

Joselyn, Sister M.   "'The Grave' as a Lyrical Short Story."   F89
<u>Studies in Short Fiction</u>, I (Spring 1964), pp. 216-221.

Contrast of the lyrical story to a "mimetic" story.   "The Grave" "focusses on a very narrow segment of action through which a universal experience...is revealed." In addition to the "syllogist plot" there is a "secondary, oscillatory movement" which involves the reader in Miranda's final vision.

--. 'On the Making of <u>Ship of Fools</u>." <u>South Dakota Review</u>, F90
I (May 1964), pp. 46-52.

An examination of the shaping of eleven separate episodes into the novel "may suggest among other things how a short-story writer is metamorphosed into a novelist, but more importantly it will show in some detail the procedures of a meticulous craftsman in action." A list of the episodes in order of publication has a corresponding description of their appearance in the novel. The additions of bridges and other passages are discussed.

<u>Jubilee</u>, X (May 1962), p. 1.   F91

An untitled interview accompanying the cover portrait of Miss Porter, about <u>Ship of Fools</u>.

Kaplan, Charles. "True Witness: Katherine Anne Porter."   F92
<u>Colorado Quarterly</u>, VII (Winter 1959), pp. 319-327.

An examination of Miss Porter's stories issued in <u>The Old Order</u> (Harcourt Brace, 1958).

"Katherine A. Porter Gives Books, Grant, to Md. U. Li-   F93
brary." Washington <u>Post</u>, December 16, 1966, Sec. C., p. 1.

Miss Porter presents manuscripts, letters, notes and her book collection to the library. She will give yearly grants to "struggling young writers to continue with their work. "

"Katherine Anne Porter Dedicates Library Room. " University   F94
of Maryland Diamondback, May 12, 1968, pp. 1, 3.

Miss Porter was honored in an afternoon and evening program on the occasion of the dedication of the Katherine Anne Porter
room of the McKeldin Library.

"Katherine Anne Porter Wins Medal. " Publisher's Weekly,   F95
CXXVII (April 13, 1940), p. 1490.

Miss Porter received the gold medal for literary achievement from the Society for the Libraries of New York University.

"Katherine Porter at Liege U. " New York Times, October   F96
29, 1954, p. 3.

Announcement of Miss Porter's appointment to the Chair of
American Civilization at Leige University as Fulbright professor。

"Katherine Porter Cited for Writings. " New York Times,   F97
October 11, 1962, p. 45.

Miss Porter receives the award of the Emerson-Thoreau
Medal of the American Academy of Arts and Sciences for her contribution to prose fiction.

Kiely, Robert.   "The Craft of Despondency: the Traditional   F98
Novelists. " Daedalus, XCII (Spring 1963), pp. 220-237.

Comparison of Evelyn Waugh, Graham Greene and Miss Porter as novelists who are "austere allegorists of a peculiarly modern
kind. " The author feels that "after reading Waugh, Porter and the
recent Greene, the extent of their devotion to literary convention is,
in part, a measure of their disaffection with human nature...if
most men cannot be saved, at least a few can be civilized. "

Kirstein, Lincoln.   "To Yell with Hale。 " New Republic,   F99
LXVII (May 27, 1931), p. 48.

A letter defending The Hound and Horn as a progressive

magazine. Miss Porter is mentioned as a contributor.

Kramer, Dale. "Notes on Lyricism and Symbols in 'The   F100
Grave'." Studies in Short Fiction, II (Summer 1965), pp. 331-336.
          Criticism of Sister M. Joselyn's study of "The Grave"
(F89): "It is not her definition but her analysis of Porter's story
that needs expansion."

Lawrence, Wes. Cleveland Plain Dealer, September 18,   F101
1965, p. 13.
          Mention of The Collected Stories of Katherine Anne Porter
in which "Miss Porter clears up the oft debated question of who
discovered her. It was, she says, Carl Van Doren...."

--. Cleveland Plain Dealer, September 25, 1965, p. 13.   F102
          Mention of Miss Porter's plea to 'not call my short novels
novelletes, or even worse, novellas" in the introduction to The Collected Stories.

"Letters by Writers Are Given to NYU by Francis Stelof."   F103
New York Times, June 21, 1965, p. 26.
          The collection of letters from Henry Miller, James Joyce
and Miss Porter were collected over a period of forty-five years.

Liberman, M.M. "Responsibility of the Novelists: The   F104
Critical Reception of Ship of Fools." Criticism, VIII (Fall 1966),
pp. 377-388.
          Two reviews (I139 and I199) are used as touchtones in ana-
lyzing critical reaction, and then the novel is discussed as an
"apologue" rather than a novel.

--. "The Short Story as Chapter in 'Ship of Fools'."   F105
Criticism, X (Winter 1968), pp. 65-71.
          A study which argues that Ship of Fools is not to be judged
as a novel. Paul W. Miller's "argument-from-genre"--that the
book should satisfy the expectations, particularly in characterization,

of a novel--is criticized (F118). "Because Ship of Fools combines
a series of 'stories,' and, overall, employs the shape of the short
story, it is to that degree like a short story in that it strives for
a single effect. But, because it only resembles a short story and
is in fact something else, it strives for that effect many times in
many combinations of characters and in greater degrees of dramatic
intensity until its conclusion."

"Library Picks Literary Aids." New York Times, May 29,   F106
1963, p. 40.

    Miss Porter and others were named honorary consultants in
American Letters at the Library of Congress.

"Mlle Passports: Contributors to this Issue." Mademoiselle, F107
XLI (July 1955), p. 20.

    Biographical note which mentions "a personal poetry anthol-
ogy...based on courses she gave at U. of Michigan" being prepared
by Miss Porter. Also mentioned is the sale of 8,000 of her Marriage is Belonging, since Mademoiselle published it in 1951.

"Mlle Passports...." Mademoiselle, XLVI (November 1957),   F108
p. 68.

    Comment on the writing of Miss Porter's poem which ap-
pears in this issue. Also mentioned is a Caedmon recording of
Miss Porter's reading of three short stories: "The Downward Path
to Wisdom," "Noon Wine," and "Pale Horse, Pale Rider."

"Mlle Passports...." Mademoiselle, XLVII (July 1958),   F109
p. 6.

    Biographical note about Miss Porter "who follows William
Faulkner as writer-in-residence at the University of Virginia this
fall." Also mentioned is an April appearance on Camera Three in
New York.

Male, Roy. "The Story of the Mysterious Stranger in Amer- F110
ican Fiction." Criticism, III (Fall 1961), pp. 281-294 /283, 286-

287/.

Discusses "Noon Wine" along with Hawthorne's "The Gray Champion," Melville's "The Lightening-Rod Man" and The Confidence-man, Harte's "The Luck of Roaring Camp," Howell's A Traveller from Altruria, and Twain's The Mysterious Stranger and "The Man that Corrupted Hadleyburg" as works that can be classified together because they represent similar action.

Marsden, Malcolm M. "Love as Threat in Katherine Anne   F111
Porter's Fiction." Twentieth Century Literature, XIII (March 1967),
pp. 29-38.

Discussion of the short stories and the novel. The stories are divided into groups: those "in which those who love in a normal pattern through purgation and renewal...those in which a defective link makes renewal impossible" and "a third kind of story /which/ depicts what happens when a character's fear of extinction is so excessive that he insulates himself emotionally from all human contact." Ship of Fools illustrates "the ways in which man has failed to reconcile his need to share his life peaceably with his instinctive need to resist a threat to his existence."

Marshall, Margaret. "Writers in the Wilderness: Katherine   F112
Anne Porter." Nation, CL (April 13, 1940), pp. 473-475.

A biographical and critical discussion of Miss Porter as an artist of limited production. "The 'promising' stage of her development was never exhibited. What we have is the finished product." Laurence Sterne and the Russian novelists are mentioned as early influences.

Matthiessen, Francis Otto. "That True and Human World."   F113
Accent, V (Winter 1945), pp. 121-123.

Discussion of the "searching originality of /Miss Porter's/ content." "The Grave" illustrates that "discoveries of the living intricacy in any relationship are Miss Porter's most recurrent resource." "The Circus" shows "the violence which lies in the heart of her discoveries." Violence is used to "reveal ethical values"

in "Noon Wine." Environment in "The Leaning Tower" and "Pale
Horse, Pale Rider" is discussed. (E37).

McGrory, Mary. Washington Sunday Star, April 12, 1953,   F114
p. E 9.
        Miss Porter's views on congressional inquiries into univer-
sity life.

McIntyre, John P. "Ship of Fools and Its Publicity, "   F115
Thought, XXXVII (Summer 1963), pp. 211-220.
        A survey of some of the publicity and criticism of the novel
which laments the substitution of personal taste for principles of
literary criticism. Literary precedents for Miss Porter's thematic
concerns are seen in Hawthorne's concern with "the leveling quality
of the rationalistic temper" and Melville's thematic and structural
concerns, particularly in The Confidence Man.

McMillan, James B. "K.A.P. Was Here." Alabama Alumni F116
News, XCV (March-April 1964), pp. 4-5, 11.
        A report of Miss Porter's appearances at the Festival of
Arts. She spoke of Ship of Fools and the critics' reaction to it.

Mexican Life, November 1930.   F117
        Mention of Miss Porter in Mexico City where she is "finish-
ing a novel...called 'Thieves Market'. "

Miller, Paul W. "Katherine Anne Porter's Ship of Fools,   F118
A Masterpiece Manqué. " University Review, XXXII (December
1965), pp. 151-157.
        A study of the deficiencies of Ship of Fools as a novel.
"Only a work that is remarkably compelling on other formal
grounds--Joyce's Ulysses, for example--can significantly modify
a form of literature by its departure from the traditional form...
I do not believe Ship of Fools is such a work. "

Molz, Kathleen. "Presenting a Fellow Passenger." PLA   F119

Bulletin, XVIII (Summer 1962), p. 9.

"Mr. O'Brien's Short-Story Selections for 1933." New York   F120
Times Book Review, July 2, 1933, p. 6.
        A review of Mr. O'Brien's The Best Short Stories of 1933
which finds "on the credit side, 'The Cracked Looking Glass' by
Katherine Anne Porter."

"N B A 1966." Newsweek, LXVII (March 28, 1966), p. 105.   F121
        Article about the presentation of the National Book Award to
Miss Porter.

Nathan, Paul S. "Rights and Permissions." Publisher's   F122
Weekly, CXXVI (November 22, 1952), p. 2098.
        A review of Miss Porter's career in writing for the screen
and an interview about her writing. "With MGM finally reported as
putting "Young Bess" into production, its /sic/ looks as though
some of the writing done in Hollywood by Katherine Anne Porter
may at last reach the screen."

Newquist, Roy. "An Interview with Katherine Anne Porter."   F123
McCall's, XCII (August 1965), pp. 88-89.
        Discussion of Miss Porter's education, teaching, views on
Henry Miller's Tropic of Cancer, art, writing, and other subjects.

New York Herald Tribune, February 5, 1945, p. 16.   F124
        Announcement that Miss Porter has been signed by MGM to
a writing contract.

New York Times, February 10, 1944, p. 13.   F125
        Announcement that Miss Porter has joined the staff of the
Library of Congress as a Fellow in Regional American Literature
and will concentrate on the old Southwestern frontier material in
the library.

New York Times Book Review, May 21, 1933, p. 7.   F126

A review of <u>Twentieth Century Short Stories</u> edited by Sylvia
Chatfield Bates which suggests "that she has neglected some of the
very newest and most promising of our American writers--Katherine
Anne Porter...."

O'Connor, William Van. "The Novel of Experience."   F127
<u>Critique</u>, I (Spring 1956), pp. 37-44.

Comparison of Henry James, Edith Wharton, Miss Porter
and Caroline Gordon. 'Old Mortality" and "Pale Horse, Pale
Rider" illustrate Miss Porter's preoccupation "with life as commonplace experience, compromise, and reconciliation with hard circumstances."

"On 'Ship of Fools'." <u>Commentary</u>, XXV (March 1963), pp.   F128
247-250.

A "Letters from Readers" reaction to Mr. Solotaroff's article (I199).

Perry, Robert L. "Porter's 'Hacienda' and the Theme of   F129
Change." <u>Midwest Quarterly</u>, VI (Summer 1965), pp. 403-415.

Discussion of "Hacienda" as art rather than a factual account of Miss Porter's experiences in Mexico. James Johnson's
suggestion that the story is an amalgam of Miss Porter's themes
(F87) is discussed.

Pierce, Marvin. "Point of View: Katherine Anne Porter's   F130
'Noon Wine'." <u>Ohio University Review</u>, III (1961), pp. 95-113.

A study of point of view in the eight scenes in 'Noon Wine."
"The shifting point of view has functioned to allow us to probe into
Mr. Thompson's character" and is the key to the story.

Plante, Patricia R. 'Katherine Anne Porter: Misanthrope   F131
Acquitted." <u>Xavier University Studies</u>, II (December 1963), pp. 87-
91.

A defense of Miss Porter who is charged with misanthropy
in Stanley Kauffmann's review of <u>Ship of Fools</u> (I166): "Could not

Criticism--Articles

the source of this outcry against mortal ugliness and weakness be
an intellectual vision of divine possibility and promise?"

"The Poet as Hero." Times Literary Supplement, March 1, F132
1957, p. 128.
    An article about Ranier Maria Rilke which mentions Miss
Porter's essay about him.

Poss, S.H. "Variations on a Theme in Four Short Stories F133
of Katherine Anne Porter." Twentieth Century Literature, IV
(April-July 1958), pp. 21-29.
    Consideration of "Circus," "Old Mortality," "Pale Horse,
Pale Rider," and "The Grave" as four stages in the life of Miranda
who discovers she is an outsider and accepts that fact. "The
Grave" is emphasized.

Powers, James F. "She Stands Alone." Four Quarters, F134
XIII (November 1962), p. 56.
    A paragraph of tribute in the Katherine Anne Porter Issue.

Prager, Leonard. "Getting and Spending: Porter's 'Theft'." F135
Perspective, XI (Winter 1960), pp. 230-234.
    Interpretation of "Theft" as "a symbolic summary of the
heroine's spiritual life." The heroine is anonymous "because of
her inability to claim herself for herself."

Publisher's Weekly, CXVIII (October 11, 1930), p. 1747. F136
    "The short stories of Katherine Anne Porter, appearing in
Hound and Horn, Century, and the Second American Caravan, at-
tracted the attention of the most discriminating of readers." The
limited edition of Flowering Judas "is now completely sold out."
"Thieves' Market" is mentioned as a novel that "will be brought
out by Harcourt, Brace next year."

"Pulitzer Drama Prize Omitted, Schlesinger's '1000 Days' F137
Wins." New York Times, May 3, 1966, pp. 1, 42.

Announcement of the winners of the Pulitzer Prize. Miss
Porter's award in fiction was for The Collected Stories of Katherine
Anne Porter.

"Recent Southern Fiction: A Panel Discussion." Katherine   F138
Anne Porter, Flannery O'Connor, Caroline Gordon, Madison Jones,
Louis D. Rubin, Jr., Moderator." Macon, Georgia: Wesleyan
College, October 28, 1960.

Rees, Richard. "Lady Chatterley." Encounter, XIV (April   F139
1960), p. 87.
    A letter which comments on Miss Porter's article "A Wreath
for the Gamekeeper," February 1960, pp. 69-77.

Ruoff, James. "Katherine Anne Porter Comes to Kansas."   F140
Midwest Quarterly, IV (Summer 1963), pp. 305-314.
    An interview by a group of faculty and students at the Uni-
versity of Wichita about the writing of the short stories and on how
to become a writer.

-- and Del Smith. "Katherine Anne Porter on Ship of Fools."F141
College English, XXIV (February 1963), pp. 396-397.
    An interview in which Miss Porter answers questions on the
background and meaning of the novel. Questions concerned the
changes that may have been made, the difficulty in completing the
novel, and the bearing of Miss Porter's changing view of the world
on the novel.

Ryan, Marjorie. "Dubliners and the Stories of Katherine   F142
Anne Porter." American Literature, XXXI (January 1960), pp.
464-473.
    A study of a dominant theme, "the hopelessness and futility
of many lives and moral paralysis," is found similar to the theme
of Joyce's work; but, although Miss Porter resembles Joyce in
theme and technique, her sympathy for her characters makes her
"akin to Hardy."

--. "Katherine Anne Porter: Ship of Fools and the Short   F143
Stories. " Bucknell Review, XII (March 1964), pp. 51-63.

   Comparison of the novel and the short stories. "The satiric
ironical undertones of the stories have become the dominant tones
of the novel: the dominant lyrical, poetic tones of the stories have
become the undertones of the novel. " Other studies and reviews
are commented on (F75 and I199).

S., B.K. Book-of-the-Month Club News, November 1944,   F144
p. 29.

   Comments about the day The Leaning Tower came out.

Schorer, Mark. "Mark Schorer's Shelf. " Bookweek Paper-   F145
back Issue, January 12, 1964, p. 4.

   Pale Horse, Pale Rider would be his choice for 1938, in a
list of books he would choose.

Schwartz, Edward Greenfield. "The Fictions of Memory. "   F146
Southwest Review, XLV (Summer 1960), pp. 204-215.

   A study of the realizations made in some of the stories.
Miranda's "initiation, conflict and survival" in "The Circus, " "Old
Mortality, " "Pale Horse, Pale Rider, " and "The Grave"; awareness
and illumination in "Flowering Judas" and "The Jilting of Granny
Weatherall"; truth in "the dumb show of the unconscious" in "Pale
Horse, Pale Rider"; recovering of order through consciousness in
"The Grave. "

--. "Katherine Anne Porter, A Critical Bibliography. "   F147
Bulletin of the New York Public Library, LVII (May 1953), pp.
211-247.

   "This bibliography is divided into two parts: the first con-
sists of an attempt at a comprehensive listing of Katherine Anne
Porter's books, stories, poems, essays, and book reviews; the
second, of critical articles and reviews of Miss Porter's work. "
Most entries are annotated. Introduction by Robert Penn Warren
(F169).

--.   "The Way of Dissent: Katherine Anne Porter's Critical   F148
Position. "   Western Humanities Review, VIII (Spring 1954), pp.
119-130.

An interpretation of Miss Porter's critical opinions about
writing, art, and her own artistic preoccupations, with quotations
from essays in The Days Before.

Slocum, Kathleen.   "Katherine Anne Porter: A Fiercely   F149
Burning Particle. "   The Censor, IV (Fall 1961), pp. 5-15.

Discussion of the themes in the short stories which are
divided into two groups: the Miranda and the non-Miranda stories.
The theme of the first group "centers on the individual and his discovery of himself"; the second "concerns individuals caught up in
the social and political upheavals of their time. "   "Circus, " 'Old
Mortality" and "Pale Horse, Pale Rider" are discussed.

Smith, Harrison.   "Writers as Readers. "   Saturday Review,   F150
XXXVI (November 28, 1953), p. 64.

Mention of Miss Porter's reading of selections from "Flowering Judas" on a Columbia LP (SL190): "Of all the Americans,
Katherine Anne Porter's rendition...is the most successful. "

Smith, J. Oates.   "Porter's Noon Wine: a Stifled Tragedy. "   F151
Renascence, XVII (Spring 1965), pp. 157-162.

A study of 'Noon Wine. ' "The secret theme of most of Porter's writing seems to be the isolation of the human heart. "   Mr.
Thompson accepts his isolation "only after intense struggle. "
"Flowering Judas" and "Pale Horse, Pale Rider" are also mentioned.

Smith, Rebecca W.   "The Southwest in Fiction. "   Saturday   F152
Review, XXV (May 16, 1942), pp. 13, 37.

Miss Porter is mentioned as a writer who portrays the
Southwest, but "the elusive beauty of Katherine Anne Porter's art
belongs to no section. "

Sobel, Louis. New York Journal American, April 10, 1962,   F153
p. 23.

    Mention of the purchase of Ship of Fools by Ray Stark "for
his own independent set up."

Southern, Terry. "Recent Fiction, Part I: When the Film   F154
Gets Good...." The Nation, CXCV (November 17, 1962), p. 330.

    A brief mention of Ship of Fools in an article which laments
the quality of recent fiction, especially novels "written as though
they were supposed to be nothing more or less than good movies..
.."

Stallman, Robert W. "Collecting Katherine Anne Porter."   F155
Four Quarters, XIII (November 1962), p. 56.

    Comments about Miss Porter's participation in the University
of Connecticut Writers Conference.

Stein, William Bysshe. "'Theft': Porter's Politics of   F156
Modern Love." Perspective, XI (Winter 1960), pp. 223-238.

    A discussion of "two submerged biblical allusions (I Peter
1:15 and Rev. 3:3) and of "Porter's view on the decline of traditional
religious authority" in "Theft."

Sutherland, Donald. "Ole Woman River: A Correspondence   F157
with Katherine Anne Porter." Sewanee Review, LXXIV (Summer
1966), pp. 754-767.

    Letters to Miss Porter, her replies, a note to Dr. Donald
Gallup of Yale University Library about Miss Porter and Gertrude
Stein, and part of a letter from Miss Stein about Miss Porter's
nephew.

Sylvester, William A. "Selected and Critical Bibliography F158
of the Uncollected Works of Katherine Anne Porter." Bulletin of
Bibliography, XIX (January 1947), p. 36.

    Short list of eighteen items. "This list purports to be ar-
ranged in order of interest from the 'belletristic' point of view."

Thompson, Barbara. "Katherine Anne Porter: An Inter-   F159
view." Paris Review, XXIX (Winter-Spring 1963), pp. 87-114.

 An interview in Miss Porter's Georgetown home. She discusses her youthful readings, the tradition in her work, her early
career, Mexico, and some of her stories (E68).

Thompson, Ralph. "Books of the Times." New York Times, F160
January 30, 1937, p. 15.

 Discussion of the voting for the Book-of-the-Month Club
Award. "It was clear almost from the start that Robinson Jeffers,
Katherine Anne Porter and James T. Farrell were the choice of
the majority...."

"Top US Scientist, Writers Honored at Dinner in White   F161
House." Boston Herald, April 30, 1962, pp. 1, 6.

 Miss Porter is listed as among those present.

Van Gelder, Robert. "Katherine Anne Porter at Work."   F162
New York Times Book Review, April 14, 1940, p. 20.

 An interview about Miss Porter's writing, written during
her residence at Baton Rouge, Louisiana (E69).

--. New York Times Book Review, November 28, 1943,   F163
p. 16.

 Mention of Miss Porter's writing about Henry James in the
Henry James Number of the Kenyon Review.

Van Zyl, John. "Surface Elegance, Grotesque Content: a   F164
Note on the Short Stories of Katherine Anne Porter." English
Studies in Africa, IX (September 1966), pp. 168-175.

 A discussion of paradox in Miss Porter's fiction. The early
short stories are more successful than Ship of Fools because their
length is more appropriate to her use of paradox. Tension is
created by opposing the grotesque and macabre with a surface elegance. "Flowering Judas," "The Old Order," "The Leaning Tower,"
"Pale Horse, Pale Rider," "Noon Wine" and the novel are discussed.

"Voices of Authors." Life, XXXV (October 12, 1953), p. 134. F165

Portrait of Miss Porter and a quotation from her recording

of "Flowering Judas."

Walsh, Chad. "A Medley of Versemakers." Bookweek,   F166

December 29, 1963, p. 10.

Comparison of the reception of Mary McCarthy's The Group

with the reception of Ship of Fools the year before. Miss Porter's

novel was "unmeritedly fawned over...as a novel of profound state-

ment and cosmic scope...."

Walsh, Thomas F. "The 'Noon Wine' Devils." Georgia   F167

Review, XXII (Spring 1968), p. 90.

Discussion of the "similarities of the Faustian pattern in

'The Devil and Daniel Webster' by Stephen Vincent Benét and 'Noon

Wine'." Benét's work is not concerned with justice while Miss Por-

ter's is.

Walton, Gerald. "Katherine Anne Porter's Use of Quakerism F168

in Ship of Fools." University of Mississippi Studies in English,

VII (1966), pp. 15-23.

A study of David's actions based on the "opinion that all of

David's actions are possibly caused by what he calls his 'Quaker

conscience'."

Warren, Robert Penn. Introduction to "Katherine Anne   F169

Porter: A Critical Bibliography." (F146)

Discussion of Miss Porter's art centering around "Flowering

Judas," which illustrates the "obviously poetic strain" and 'Noon

Wine," which illustrates the "exceptional precision of her language."

--. "Katherine Anne Porter (Irony with a Center)."   F170

Kenyon Review, IV (Winter 1942), pp. 29-42.

A study of paradox in the short stories. "Flowering Judas"

illustrates a paradox of moral realities; 'Old Mortality," the para-

dox of fact and myth; 'Noon Wine," paradox of motives; "The

Cracked Looking Glass," a complex of paradoxes. Irony is not
used for its sake but to affirm "the constant need for exercising
discrimination..." (E74, E75, E76).

Waugh, Doris. "The Ninth Annual Arts Forum Program   F171
Gets Underway on Thursday Morning, March 13." The Carolinian,
XXXII (March 7, 1952), pp. 1, 2, 3.

Announcement that Miss Porter "will be guest critic of stu-
dent writing from seven colleges this year."

Welty, Eudora. "The Eye of the Story." Yale Review, LV   F172
(Winter 1966), pp. 265-274.

A discussion of Miss Porter's writing about the interior of
our lives, where her stories take place. Miss Porter uses "memory imagery...her subject is what lies beneath the surface."

Wescott, Glenway. "Katherine Anne Porter: The Making   F173
of a Novel." Atlantic, CCIX (April 1962), pp. 42-49.

An essay about Miss Porter's life and writing, particularly
Ship of Fools. An expanded version of the essay appears in Wes-
cott's Images of Truth (E79), a briefer version in Book-of-the-
Month Club News (I207).

West, Ray B. "Katherine Anne Porter and 'Historic Mem-   F174
ory'." Hopkins Review, VI (Fall 1952), pp. 16-27.

An analysis of Miss Porter's methods of writing from memory. "Old Mortality" is considered at length (E83, E84).

--. "Katherine Anne Porter: Symbol and Theme in 'Flower- F175
ing Judas'." Accent, VII (Spring 1947), pp. 182-188.

Examination of "Flowering Judas," with the aim of understanding just what the author means by social sensibility...how it
operates within the story itself." Three types of symbolism are
discussed (E86, E87).

"Who's Who in the Library of Congress--Miss Katherine   F176

Anne Porter." Library of Congress Information Bulletin, February-March, 1944, p. 5.

Biographical sketch of Miss Porter "who has just been appointed Resident Fellow of the Library of Congress in Regional American Literature."

Wiesenfarth, Brother Joseph. "Illusion and Allusion: Re-   F177 flections in 'The Cracked Looking Glass'." Four Quarters, XII (November 1962), pp. 30-37.

A discussion of the story as one of a "dreamer whose every day is spent in anticipation of 'something great...going to happen,' but who must finally admit that each of her days has been" a disappointment.

"Winners Press Conference: Remarks." Publisher's Weekly, F178 CXCIX (March 28, 1966), pp. 30-32.

Summary of Miss Porter's answers to questions at the press conference for National Book Award Winners.

Winsten, Archer. "Presenting the Portrait of an Artist."   F179 New York Post, May 6, 1937, p. 17.

An interview prompted by the Book-of-the-Month Club Award "said by Miss Porter to be, with one exception, the only time she's ever been interviewed."

Wolfe, Peter. "The Problems of Granny Weatherall."   F180 College Language Association Journal, XI (December 1967), pp. 142-148.

Analysis of the story centering around the idea that 'Ellen Weatherall was pregnant at the time of her jilting."

"Writing A Prize Story is Easy--to Miss Porter." New   F181 York Herald Tribune, April 6, 1940, p. 8.

An interview after Miss Porter won the gold medal of the Society for the Libraries of New York University. Her work on 'No Safe Harbor" and "The Devil and Cotton Mather" is discussed.

Young, Vernon A. "The Art of Katherine Anne Porter."   F182
New Mexico Quarterly, XV (Autumn 1945), pp. 326-341.

An article which responds to the critical acclaim of The
Leaning Tower as belated and misplaced.

Youngblood, Sarah. "Structure and Imagery in Katherine   F183
Anne Porter's 'Pale Horse, Pale Rider'." Modern Fiction Studies,
V (Winter 1959-1960), pp. 344-352.

An article in the "Southern Writers" issue about "Miss Porter's place in contemporary fiction."

G. DOCTORAL DISSERTATIONS AND MASTERS' THESES

Adams, Robert Hickman. "The Significance of Point of View   G1
in Katherine Anne Porter's Ship of Fools." Ph.D., University of
Southern California, 1964. /Abstracted in Dissertation Abstracts,
XXVI (October 1965), p. 2201/

    "Point of view serves Porter technically...to resist senti-
mentality...to unify the novel." "Point of view is as significant as
content...when it is wrapped into a disastrous manifestation of human egoism."

Graves, Allen Wallace. "Difficult Contemporary Short Stories: G2
William Faulkner, Katherine Anne Porter, Dylan Thomas, Eudora
Welty and Virginia Woolf." Ph.D., University of Washington, 1953.
/Abstracted in Dissertation Abstracts, XIV (November 1954), pp.
2067-2068/

    This study presents a method of analysis of difficult short
stories by identifying the obscurity and judging "whether it is justi-
fied artistically." "Flowering Judas," "He," and "Pale Horse, Pale
Rider" are discussed.

Hertz, Robert Neil. "Rising Waters: A Study of Katherine   G3
Anne Porter." Ph.D., Cornell University, 1964. /Abstracted in
Dissertation Abstracts, XXV (December 1964), pp. 3571-3572/

    Essays in The Days Before are examined "to determine Miss
Porter's view of the function of art and the nature of experience"
in order to discover her interest in the "'essence' of man's motives
and personality." Her concern with human conflict is examined in
the short stories. Ship of Fools is examined as a philosophical
novel and for the relationship of the whole novel to the two climac-
tic events of the story.

Krishnamurthi, Matighatti G. "Katherine Anne Porter: A   G4
Study in Themes." Ph.D., University of Wisconsin, 1966. /Ab-
stracted in Dissertation Abstracts, XXVIII (August 1967), pp. 682-A-
683-A/

    Recurring themes are explored in different works. "The fic-
tion...is interpreted as her sustained attempts to understand and in-

terpret" both the problems of modern man and his failure to find solutions.

Ledbetter, Nan Wilson Thompson. "The Thumbprint: A G5
Study of People in Katherine Anne Porter's Fiction." Ph.D., University of Texas, 1966. [Abstracted in Dissertation Abstracts, XXVIII (December 1967), pp. 2252-A - 2253-A]
"A discussion of selected characters, chosen as representatives in Miss Porter's fiction." The characters "fall into groups representing certain themes which she has found basic to the human condition...." The initiation theme, the theme of self-delusion, the theme of moral definition and the quest theme are discussed.

Murphy, Edward F. "Henry James and Katherine Anne Porter: G6*
Endless Relations." Ph.D., University of Ottawa, 1959.

Nance, Brother William Leslie, S.N. "The Principle of Re- G7
jection: A Study of the Thematic Unity in the Fiction of Katherine Anne Porter." Ph.D., University of Notre Dame, 1963. [Abstracted in Dissertation Abstracts, XXIV (September 1963), pp. 1172-1173]
A study of the principle of rejection "which is the central impulse in the fiction of Katherine Anne Porter" (E41).

Redden, Dorothy Sue. "The Legend of Katherine Anne Por- G8
ter." Ph.D., Stanford University, 1965. [Abstracted in Dissertation Abstracts, XXVI (May 1966), pp. 6722-6723]
A study of the "unifying themes" which center around Miranda, whose life is divided into a "pre-crisis period," "the crisis," and "the post-crisis period." "This examination clarifies Miss Porter's insistent theme of alienation."

Schwartz, Edward. "The Fiction of Katherine Anne Porter." G9*
Ph.D., Syracuse, 1953 (F147).

Sexton, Katherine Adams. "Katherine Anne Porter's Years G10* in Denver." M.A., Colorado University, 1951.

Stalling, Donald. 'Katherine Anne Porter: Life and Liter-   G11*
ary Mirror." M.A., Texas Christian University, 1951.

Waldrip, Louise. "A Bibliography of the Works of Katherine   G12
Anne Porter." Ph.D., University of Texas, 1967. ⟦Abstracted in
Dissertation Abstracts, XXVII (June 1967), p. 4269-A⟧
    Descriptive listing of Miss Porter's works, 1917-1964.

Yosha, Lee William. "The World of Katherine Anne Porter." G13
Ph.D., University of Michigan, 1961. ⟦Abstracted in Dissertation
Abstracts, XXI (June 1961), pp. 3795-3796⟧
    A study of "the formal and ideological structures" of Miss
Porter's stories. The study concludes that the stories "demonstrate
the furthest degree to which the techniques of the short story have
been developed" and that "her themes originate in the internal world
of human proclivities, work through human character, and move
outward into the external world of human action."

H. FOREIGN LANGUAGE MATERIAL

Antonini, Ciacomo. "Un Gross Romanzo di Katherine Porter." H1
Fiera Letteraria, XVII (November 11, 1962), pp. 1-2.

v. Borch, Herbert. "'Die Deutschen sind allsumal grausam,   H2
boese und Fanatisch' /Dokument des Hasses: K. A. Porters 'Narrenschiff'." Die Welt, June 9, 1962.

Cameron, Phil. "Writers of the American South." Amerpʌka, H3
X, pp. 18-20.
    "This article discusses the work of three Southern writers
who, in the words of William Faulkner, write of the heart and not
of the glands."

Connolly, Francis X. "Lettre de New York." La Table   H4
Ronde, CLXXVI (September 1962), pp. 88-92.

"Das Narrenschiff." Der Spiegel, September 12, 1962, pp.   H5
74-77.

Galey, Matthieu. "Katherine Porter." Arts (Paris), CMXXIX H6
(December 4-10, 1963), p. 3.

Gorlier, Claudia. "Tre Esperience Narrative." Gallaria   H7
(Italy), IV (1954), pp. 349-359.

Holthusen, Hans E. "Un Bateau-libre. (a Propos de La Nef   H8
des fous)." Preuves, CLXII, pp. 80-83.

Kanters, Robert. "Mon Beau Navire, O Ma Memoire."   H9
Figaro Littéraire, XXVI (December 26, 1963-January 1, 1964), p. 4.

Leitzmann, Sabina. "Eine Allegorie von der deutchen Gefahr/ H10
Der neu Amerikanische Bestseller 'Narrenschiff' von Katherine Anne
Porter." Frankfurter Allgemeine Zeitung, July 16, 1962, p. 16.

Muhlen, Norbert. "Deutsche, wie sie im Buche Stehen." Der H11

Criticism--Foreign

<u>Monat</u>, December 1962, pp. 38-45.

Paechter, Heinz. "Miss Porters neue Kleider/Missverstaend- H12
nisse um einen Amerikanischen Bestseller." <u>Deutsche Zeitung</u>,
October 13-14, 1962.

Shapiro, Karl. "Pisarae Uoza Twórczoŝci Literackry."   H13
<u>Amery</u>, NR 15, pp. 12-13.

"Un Nouvelle de Katherine Anne Porter: 'Le Viel Homme'."   H14
<u>Les Nouvelles Littéraries</u>. February 24, 1955, p. 1.

I. BOOK REVIEWS

KATHERINE ANNE PORTER'S FRENCH SONG BOOK

"French Song-Book." New York Herald Tribune (Paris), De-   I1
cember 25, 1933, p. 5.

"To an American or a Briton who knows French children's
songs this book is a perfect delight."

Poetry, XLIII (February 1934), p. 290.   I2

"Although the book is too expensive for popular circulation,
we can imagine no more delightful edition of such classics...."

Root, Waverly Lewis. "Poet and Printer Vie in Adorning Old   I3
French Airs." Chicago Daily Tribune (Paris), November 27, 1933,
p. 2.

"To read Miss Porter's translations one would never dream
that so much effort was necessary, for they appear to have been
born spontaneously."

HACIENDA

Baker, Howard. "Some Notes on New Fiction." Southern Re-   I4
view, I (1935), pp. 188-189.

Miss Porter is praised for her ability to capture "the elusive
properties of people and things." It is noted that she seldom
writes "an extended dialogue or a dramatically complete scene."

"Books: Some Christmas Suggestions." New Yorker, X (De-   I5
cember 1934), pp. 140-141 /141/.

"'Hacienda,' by Katherine Anne Porter, which means it's
distinguished work."

Chamberlain, John. "Books of the Times." New York Times,   I6
December 10, 1934, p. 19.

"Miss Porter's story, offered in a small first edition of
895 copies, contains some first-rate writing." The story is compared to Erna Fergusson's Fiesta in Mexico.

Cowley, Malcolm. "Books in Review." New Republic,   I7

174   Katherine Anne Porter
LXXIII (May 29, 1935), p. 79.
    "I wish that something by Katherine Anne Porter could be
published without limitations and distributed to an undeluxified audi-
ence. "

Gannett, Lewis. "Books and Things." New York Herald   I8
Tribune, December 8, 1934, p. 13.
    "...one might have been reminded of Eisenstein's adventures
with Upton Sinclair's brother-in-law. "

Hart, Elizabeth. "Slight and Short Stories." New York   I9
Herald Tribune Books, December 16, 1934, p. 15.
    "'Hacienda' disappointed me. I can't help wondering if it is
the polished-up notes for a future novel...."

"Notes on Fiction." Nation, CXL (March 27, 1935), p. 369. I10
    "The shortness of the book is unsatisfactory, for the mater-
ial and the implications--and the manner--are not slight at all. "

P., C.G. "A New Story by Katherine Anne Porter." New   I11
York Times Book Review, December 23, 1934, p. 4.
    "In Flowering Judas Miss Porter showed with what skillful
art she could write stories.... She is unable to surpass herself
here. " Her style is compared to Kay Boyle's.

Wolfe, Bertram. "Books of the Age." Workers' Age (New   I12**
York), January 12, 1935.
    Marxist criticism of Hacienda. "Everyone seems to be there
in this little essay--everyone, that is, except the new Mexican, the
worker, the already half-awakened peasant...types that are still a
minority and were not easy for Katherine Anne Porter to meet up
with or to comprehend or to catch in her silver-filigreed prose,
but these are the ones who will end the Mexico of Eisenstein's
film and Miss Porter's book...."

FLOWERING JUDAS AND OTHER STORIES

Angoff, Charles. "An Honest Story Teller." <u>American</u>   I13
<u>Spectator</u>, III (November 1935), p. 11.

"It is...a great pleasure to come upon an author of such obvious maturity and unimpeachable honesty...." "The Cracked Looking-Glass" is considered the best story in the book.

Bogan, Louise. "Flowering Judas." <u>New Republic</u>, LXIV   I14
(October 22, 1930), pp. 277-278.

"Its excellence rises directly from the probity of the conception" (E9).

<u>Boston Evening Transcript Books Section</u>, October 26, 1935,   I15
p. 4.

"To those who have been looking expectantly for new stories, a new edition of the old is a disappointment."

Brown, John L. "Readers and Writers in Paris." <u>New York</u>   I16
<u>Times Book Review</u>, March 3, 1946, p. 14.

The recent French edition of <u>Flowering Judas</u> "is receiving appreciative reviews."

Chamberlain, John. "Books of the Times." New York   I17
<u>Times</u>, October 11, 1935, p. L 23.

"Whenever a professional yearner for the good old days bemoans the lack of good prose in this vulgar modern world, I always think of Katherine Anne Porter."

--. "The Short Story Muddles On." <u>New Republic</u>, LXV   I18
(January 7, 1931), pp. 225-226.

In a book review of five collections of short stories, Miss Porter is mentioned in answer to the question, "How can stories become something more than literary exercises of one sort or another?"

Clark, Eleanor. "Cameos." <u>New Republic</u>, LXXXV (Decem-   I19 ber 25, 1935), p. 207.

"Miss Porter is not an easy author. Her scope is limited
and she counteracts this weakness by satire so pointed and com-
pressed and such perfection of style that one is sometimes forced
to concentrate more on word patterns than on the substance of a
story. "

Christian Century, LII (November 6, 1935), p. 1426.   I20
"It is remarkably good stuff. "

"Complexity and Depth. " Saturday Review, XII (December   I21
14, 1935), p. 16.
'Her style...is beautiful and individual and her material
chosen with care for its rarity, its drama, or its exoticism. "

Dawson, Margaret Cheney. "A Perfect Flowering. " New   I22
York Herald Tribune Books, September 14, 1930, pp. 3-4.
Miss Porter "writes her reports as an artist, and their
clarity is not marred by her sense of beauty or her compassion. "

Dickson, Thomas. "Absorbing Characters. " New York Daily   I23
News, October 13, 1935, p. 84.
"Miss Porter has learned a great deal from Maugham about
the short story, but in this collection she demonstrates that she is
able to stand firm on her feet. "

"Fiction. " Booklist, XXXII (December 1935), p. 110.   I24
'Delicate precision of style, combined with clarity and econ-
omy.... "

"'Flowering Judas' and Other Recent Works of Fiction. " New   I25
York Times Book Review, September 28, 1930, p. 6.
Miss Porter is considered a member of a group including
Malcolm Cowley, Elizabeth Madox Roberts, Glenway Wescott, Yvor
Winters and Kenneth Burke who write with care.

Higgins, Cecile. "Short Stories." New York Sun, October   I26
26, 1935, p. 10.

"...one's knowledge of human nature will be appreciably en-
riched, and one's respect for the short story as a work of art
doubly confirmed after reading 'Flowering Judas and Other Stories'."

"Mexican Contrasts." Times Literary Supplement, April 18,   I27
1936, p. 333.

The stories "rely rather too exclusively on the assumption
that the meanderings of the mind are interesting enough to dis-
pense the artist from imposing a pattern upon them."

Nashe, Anne. "A Vivid Awareness." Carmel, Cal. Pacific   I28
Weekly, November 11, 1935, p. 226.

"Atmosphere Miss Porter can create as a painter can, and
it is atmosphere that makes these stories rare and valuable."

Nichols, Esther K. "Katherine Porter Collects." Brooklyn   I29
Daily Eagle, November 3, 1935, p. C 16.

Miss Porter's style "is as parsimonious as anything I have
ever read and it makes laconic writers like Hemingway and Kay
Boyle seem spendthrifts by comparison."

Oakland, California Post-Enquirer, January 25, 1936.   I30**
"The style of Katherine Anne Porter is real. It is not literary exhibitionism."

Richardson, Eudora Ramsey. Bookman, XLLII (October 1930),   I31
p. 172.

'Done...with feeling for dramatic values, with clarity, with
delicate delineation of characters, and in language transcendently
beautiful."

Seldes, Gilbert. "True to Type." New York Evening   I32**
Journal, December 13, 1936.

One of "several dozen books...meritorious in the judgement

of good critics, but not financially successful. "

Tate, Allen. "A New Star. " Nation, CXXXI (October 1,   I33
1930), pp. 352-353.
    "'Flowering Judas' is not a promising book...it is a fully
matured art. "

Townsend, Anne B. Philadelphia Inquirer, December 7, 1935,   I34
p. 12.
    "She is not easy to know, but any expenditure of time and
concentration on the part of the reader brings a rich reward. "

Troy, William. "A Matter of Quality. " Nation, CXLI (Octo-   I35
ber 29, 1935), pp. 517-518.
    Miss Porter has managed to avoid "the two worst perils of
the contemporary prose writer--artificiality and that self-conscious
effort at sincerity which is a special kind of artificiality. "

Walton, Edith H. "An Exquisite Story-Teller. " New York   I36
Herald Tribune Book Review, October 3, 1935, p. 7.
    "No one who admires clarity and precision in prose will wish
to miss this book. "

--. Forum, XCIV (December 1935), p. ix.   I37
    "Clearly one of the best and most fastidious of modern short-
story writers, Miss Porter is a person to be reckoned with. "

--. "Katherine Anne Porter's Stories. " New York Times   I38
Book Review, October 20, 1935, p. 6.
    "...to say that she comes closer to Kay Boyle than to any
of her contemporaries will perhaps give some notion of Miss Porter's quality. "

"A Wide Choice for Readers in the Christmas Book Lists. "   I39
New York Times Book Review, December 1, 1935, p. 37.
    "Miss Porter has humour, vitality, and a wide range. "

Winters, Yvor. "Major Fiction." Hound and Horn, IV (Jan-   I40
uary 1931), pp. 303-305.

A mixed review-article, rather grudging of praise. "He,"
as well as "Magic," and "Rope," seems "an object of curiosity...
rather than a general symbol of experience." "Maria Concepción"
receives praise as "much richer...a technically straight narrative,
marred a little by over-decoration." "'Flowering Judas' and 'The
Jilting of Granny Weatherall' employ a convention...of revery al-
ternating with perceptions of the present" (E22).

NOON WINE

Belitt, Ben. "South Texas Primitive." Nation, CXLIV (May   I41
15, 1937), p. 57.

"Miss Porter's simplicities, in the last analysis, are strata-
gems, and the story's impact, for all its incidental rewards, is
muted by its rigors."

Morse, Samuel French. "Style Plus." Reading and Collecting, I42
I (April 1937), p. 14.

"I have read no story in a long time which left me as intense an impression...her story is a solid, finished piece of writing."

Walton, Edith H. "An Ironic Tragedy." New York Times   I43
Book Review, April 11, 1937, p. 7.

"'Noon Wine' is not as good as the best stories in 'Flowering Judas,' although it has the incidental charm inseparable from
Miss Porter's work."

PALE HORSE, PALE RIDER

Booklist, XXXV (April 13, 1939), p. 271.   I44

"Beautiful writing, of special interest for its technical
skill...."

Crume, Paul. Southwest Review, XXV (January 1940), pp.   I45
213-218.

"Miss Porter's writing will be most appreciated by those who read not for entertainment or information but for a certain esthetic satisfaction." Biographical material is included in this review-article, including Miss Porter's account of her writing My Chinese Marriage and "The Dove of Chapacalco."

Fadiman, Clifton. "Katherine Anne Porter." New Yorker,   I46 XV (April 1, 1939), pp. 77-78.

"These tales...do not strike you as 'significant,' they do not clarify our times for you, they seem to have no great scope or depth. Nevertheless, there is something firm about them, something marmoreal."

Gannett, Lewis. "Books and Things." New York Herald   I47 Tribune, March 30, 1939, p. 23.

"This is insight: this is real writing."

Hartung, Philip T. Commonweal, XXX (May 19, 1939), pp.   I48 109-110.

"With these three novelettes, Katherine Anne Porter establishes herself as a prose stylist of first rank."

Isherwood, Christopher. New Republic, XCVIII (April 19,   I49 1939), pp. 312-313.

Miss Porter is compared to Katherine Mansfield who had "genius and the failings of genius." "Miss Porter has no genius but much talent."

London Times Literary Supplement, May 27, 1939, p. 311.   I50

"What gives distinction to Mrs. Porter's work is the strain of poetry in it." However, in "Pale Horse, Pale Rider" beauty is cultivated "too assiduously."

Moult, Thomas. Manchester Guardian, June 29, 1939, p. 7.   I51

"A truly artistic collection, one that is worthy to be put alongside the writings in the same medium by...Miss Willa Cather."

North American Review, CCXLVII (Summer 1939), p. 339.   I52
    "Miss Porter's new book will solidify her already envious
position in contemporary fiction."

Pratt Institute Quarterly, Summer 1939, p. 30.   I53
    "By one of the best of contemporary short story writers."

"Promise Kept." Time, XXXIII (April 10, 1939), p. 75.   I54
    "A distinctive book, elusive as quicksilver, it has the subtle-
ty that has marked all Miss Porter's writing, none of the precious-
ness that has previously marred it."

Reid, Forest. Spectator, CLXII (June 9, 1939), p. 1010.   I55
    "Miss Porter has discovered the form which exactly suits
her particular gifts. Of course she could write a novel, yet I
doubt if on a large canvas her method would be so successful."

Rice, Philip Blair. "The Art of Katherine Anne Porter."   I56
Nation, CXLVIII (April 15, 1939), p. 442.
    "Her work so far shows that she has range and versatility
as well as polish. Of her depth I am less certain, despite the
keenness of her psychological analysis."

Rosenfeld, Paul. "An Artist in Fiction." Saturday Review, I57
XIX (April 1939), p. 7.
    "Form, invention, and poetry...distinguish the trio of tiny,
affecting novels which comprise her present volume."

S., M.W. "More Flowering." Christian Science Monitor   I58
Weekly Magazine Section, May 13, 1939, p. 10.
    "Miss Porter still writes for a select audience, for the type
of reader who enjoys, according to the old precept, not only what
the author says, but what she whispers."

Soskin, William. "Rare Beauty of Good Writing." New York I59
Herald Tribune Books, April 9, 1939, p. 5.

"The reader feels the invaluable sense of having shared
years of experience and emotional understanding with the author
long before" she wrote them down.

Stegner, Wallace. "Conductivity in Fiction." Virginia Quar-   160
terly Review, XV (Autumn 1939), pp. 444-445.
   "There is in all these three novelettes an absoluteness of
technique and a felicity of language that are seldom encountered
even in the best fiction."

Thompson, Ralph. New York Times, March 30, 1939, p. L-21.161
   "Today's volume should disappoint none of Miss Porter's
admirers."

Walton, Edith H. "The Delicate Art of Katherine Anne Por-   162
ter." New York Times Book Review, April 2, 1939, p. 5.
   "We have waited a long time, but it is worth it."

Wescott, Glenway. "Praise." Southern Review, V (No. 1,   163
1939), pp. 161-173.
   A critical and personal evaluation of Miss Porter's writings,
purposes and goals. "Noon Wine" is likened to Paradise Lost in
that Lucifer appears in each work. The volume of stories is compared to Katherine Mansfield's writing, James Joyce's early stories
and to E.M. Forster's Passage to India. "The rarity and brevity
of her publications" and the complaint that "Miss Porter's writing
has every excellence except humor" are discussed.

West, Anthony. New Statesman and Nation, XVII (May 27,   164
1939), pp. 832-833.
   Miss Porter's writing is seen as "hardly the expression of
ideas so much as a record of the emotions of a mind of exquisite
sensibility."

Wisconsin Library Bulletin, XXXV (October 1939), p. 168.   165
   Miss Porter's style and "emotional awareness" are praised.

THE ITCHING PARROT

Chamberlain, John. New York Times, March 20, 1942, p.   I66
L-23.

"The introduction is alone worth the price of the book; it is
the best background material on the last days of Spanish Mexico
that I have ever encountered."

Garnett, Emily. Library Journal, LXVII (March 1, 1942),   I67
p. 225.

"A Latin-American classic; lacing the conciseness and pic-
turesque language of Lazarello des Tormes, but, no doubt, a true
commentary on Mexico of 1800."

Jones, Howard Mumford. "Lizárdi." Saturday Review, XXV   I68
(April 4, 1942), p. 14.

Miss Porter's introduction is praised. If she were to write
with similar skill about other Mexican literary figures, she would
"do much to increase our understanding of Mexico."

New Yorker, XVIII (March 21, 1942), p. 70.   I69

"Miss Porter tells you more about the unfortunate life of
Lizárdi than most people would insist on knowing." The book itself "is rather dull."

Rugoff, Milton. New York Herald Tribune Books, March 22,   I70
1942, p. 9.

A listing under "A Selected List of Important Spring Books."

Ryan, Edwin. Commonweal, XXXVI (July 24, 1942), pp. 331-   I71
332.

"The present translation is well done, the translator having
wisely omitted passages which merely hold up the action without
contributing anything of real value."

Trilling, Lionel. "Mexican Classic." Nation, CLIV (March   I72
28, 1942), pp. 373-374.

"Miss Porter's translation is a model of firm simple prose in the manner of the eighteenth century masters of realism...."
Mr. Trilling is disturbed because he finds the book which influenced so many people a bore, and attributes his reaction, in part, to the translation.

Walton, Edith H. "Bygone World." New York Times Book   I73
Review, May 10, 1942, p. 22.
    Praise for Miss Porter's introduction "which supplies the necessary background in a most clear and telling fashion."

Wolfe, Bertram D. "Picaresque." New Republic, CVI (June   I74
12, 1942), pp. 868-870.
    "After Miss Porter's excision of the sermons...the essential kinship is close with all the picaresque novels of the past." However, her "excellent introduction" mistakenly asserts "that this work is 'almost the last of its kind'."

THE LEANING TOWER
American Mercury, LIX (December 1944), p. 766.   I75
    A brief review which summarizes the stories, finding "the title story...wordy, over-symbolical, and its point...far from clear." "The other stories are enormously better...."

Baker, Herschel. "Katherine Anne Porter's Art." Dallas,   I76
Texas Morning News, October 1, 1944, Part III, p. 12.
    "It is a great joy to welcome Miss Porter's new sheaf of short stories."

Beach, Joseph W. "Self-Consciousness and Its Antidote."   I77
Virginia Quarterly Review, XXI (Spring 1945), pp. 292-293.
    Miss Porter is "refreshingly free from self-consciousness. What she has in plenty is artistic conscience.... she is more a truth teller than a realist." The reviewer also considers John Steinbeck's Cannery Row and compares it with Miss Porter's work.

Booklist, XLI (October 1944), p. 59.   I78
   "Skillful and beautiful writing that, unfortunately, may ap-
peal to only discriminating readers."

Buckman, Gertrude. "Miss Porter's New Stories." Partisan I79
Review, XII (Winter 1945), p. 134.
   Miss Porter "consistently writes luminous prose, of an ex-
actness of choice and suggestiveness of phrasing, which is alto-
gether extraordinary." Miss Porter is briefly compared with Virginia Woolf.

Catholic World, CLX (November 1944), p. 189.   I80
   "No one who has a feeling for style can afford to miss Katherine Anne Porter."

Chicago Sun Book Week, September 24, 1944, p. 8.   I81
   "If you have read 'The Flowering Judas' or 'Pale Horse,
Pale Rider,' you will know the finished and smooth writing that you
may expect."

Christian Century, LXI (October 11, 1944), p. 1170.   I82
   "All exhibit a calculated and skillful technique...."

Downing, Francis. Commonweal, XL (September 29, 1944), I83
p. 572.
   Praise for Miss Porter's "artistic integrity." Her "sensi-
tiveness and subtlety are a tribute to the intellect and to the spirit."

Commonweal, XL (October 20, 1944), p. 20.   I84
   "A collection of short sketches which continue to reveal the
author's poetic sensibility."

Hansen, Harry. "The First Reader." New York World Tele- I85
gram, September 14, 1944, p. 22.
   "Only nine stories, written at intervals in 10 years....but
they are important on any publication day."

Jones, Howard Mumford. "A Smooth Literary Texture."   186
Saturday Review, XXVII (September 30, 1944), p. 15.

"No change of fashion can antiquate the finesse of Miss Porter's pen, whose quiet manner and deceptively simple texture have
something of the ease of Jane Austen."

Kelley, Gilbert H. Library Journal, XLIX (September 1,   187
1944), p. 699.

"Recommended." "'A Day's Work' encroaches upon James
Farrell's world...."

Kirkus, XII (September 1, 1944), pp. 378-379.   188
"Fine writing, muted, finished---for a discriminating market."

London Times Literary Supplement, November 10, 1945, p.   189
533.

A brief review in which Miss Porter is compared to Katherine Mansfield.

Molloy, Robert. "The Book of the Day." New York Sun,   190
September 15, 1944, p. 20.

"Here, in a world of aging Negro servants, strong-minded
children, and the indomnitable old grandmother, Miss Porter is at
her inimitable best...."

Morley, Christopher. Book-of-the-Month Club News, October   191
1944, p. 13.

"Like everything Miss Porter chooses to publish, this book
deserves the sensitive reader."

Prescott, Orville. New York Times, September 17, 1944,   192
p. 17.

"Admirers of her work will not want to miss 'The Leaning
Tower'." Although the stories "are very much Miss Porter's own,
the ghost of Katherine Mansfield seems to hover over them."

--. Yale Review, XXXIV (Autumn 1944), p. 190.   I93
    "A collection of nine short stories by one of the most ex-
quisite stylists and subtle and penetrating writers of our time."

Read, Martha.   "The Mind's Delineation." Quarterly Review   I94
of Literature, II (No. 2, 1945), pp. 150-152.
    "The author captures again the dramatic emotional intensity
of the stories in Pale Horse, Pale Rider." Miss Porter's stories
are compared with Katherine Mansfield's.

Saphieha, Virgilia.   "By Katherine Anne Porter." New York   I95
Herald Tribune Weekly Book Review, September 17, 1944, p. 2.
    "Miss Porter's craftsmanship...again reaches a high level
in these new stories."

Spencer, Theodore. Sewanee Review, LIII (April-June 1945),   I96
pp. 300-301.
    "In this volume there is no one story which is as fine as
her earlier 'Pale Horse, Pale Rider,' and some of the stories are
slight, little glimpses at experience with scarcely enough material
in them for a picture."

"Texas and Berlin." Time, XLIV (September 25, 1944), pp.   I97
103-104.
    "Katherine Anne Porter has become one of the intelligentsia's
most admired short-story writers."

Trilling, Diana. Nation, CLIX (September 1944), pp. 359-360. I98
    "Prose like this is not only in the best American tradition,
from Mark Twain to Hemingway, but typical of Miss Porter's constant effort to keep her eye on the object."

Warren, Robert Penn.   "Reality and Strength in These Tales." I99
Chicago Tribune Books, October 15, 1944, p. 17.
    "A body of stories distinguished for a remarkable combina-
tion of artistic poise and philosophical implication and narrative ex-

citement. "

Weeks, Edward. "Blood and Ivory. " <u>Atlantic Weekly</u>,   I100
CLXXIV (November 1944), pp. 131, 133.

    A review which expresses disappointment of expectations
aroused by <u>Flowering Judas</u>. "One must respect the sheer virtu-
ousity of Miss Porter's prose...but style without warmth, like
character without emotion, can be a tedious affair. "

Wescott, Glenway. "Stories by a Writer's Writer. " <u>New</u>   I101
<u>York Times Book Review</u>, September 17, 1944, p. 1.

    "We have no American fiction as good as what her twenty-
two sketches, stories and novelettes indicate that she might give
us. " Mr. Wescott imagines her writing "a sort of 'War and
Peace'...as if she were a little daughter or granddaughter of Tol-
stoy.... "

Whicher, George F. New York <u>Herald Tribune</u>, September   I102
14, 1944, p. 19.

    Praise for Miss Porter's stories, "if creations as delicate
and diaphanous as some of these are not maligned by so heavy a
name. "

Wilson, Edmund. "Books: Katherine Anne Porter. " <u>New</u>   I103
<u>Yorker</u> XX (September 30, 1944), pp. 72-74.

    Miss Porter is "absolutely a first-rate artist... " (A88).

Young, Marguerite. "Fictions Mystical and Epical. " <u>Kenyon</u>   I104
<u>Review</u>, VII (Winter 1945), pp. 152-154.

    Miss Porter's work is seen as "devoid of the transcendental
concept, as it is of the social, though sated with detached luminos-
ity and other-worldliness, almost enchantment. " Miss Young finds
Miss Porter's concern is with the individual's self-awareness.

THE DAYS BEFORE

Allen, Charles. Arizona Quarterly, IX (Spring 1953), pp.   I105
71-73.

"These pieces show a divided sensibility. In many areas
Miss Porter learned self-knowledge early and has managed to hold
heart and mind intact, " but the author questions her statement that
"'we also desire to be unhappy and that we create our own suffer-
ings'. "

Baker, Carlos. "A Happy Harvest. " New York Times Book   I106
Review, November 2, 1952, p. 4.
    "As rewarding as reading a fine novel. "

Booklist, XLIX (November 1, 1952), p. 86.   I107
    "The essays all bear the imprint of their author's conviction
of the high mission of the artist. "

Fiedler, Leslie A. "Love is Not Enough. " Yale Review,   I108
XLII (Spring 1953), pp. 456, 458-459.
    "Miss Porter's literary essays come embedded in a context
of panegyrics on flowers, birds and Mexico. " Her "occasional de-
partures from orthodoxy" and "her more fashionable absurdities
(the claim of greatness for the late poetry of Edith Sitwell) are con-
nected with her involvement in a tradition that has outlived its use-
fulness. " The essay also considers F.O. Matthiessen's The Re-
sponsibilities of the Critic, John Lehmann's The Open Night, and
Henry Miller's The Books in My Life.

Fremantle, Anne. "Yesterdays of Katherine Anne Porter. "   I109
Commonweal, LVII (November 7, 1952), pp. 122-123.
    A review which focuses on Miss Porter's "three views of
Miss /Gertrude/ Stein" and her treatment of Willa Cather.

Hardy, John Edward. "Interesting Essays by a Novelist. "   I110
Baltimore Evening Sun, January 20, 1953, p. 16.
    "This is a charming book. "

Hobson, Laura Z. Saturday Review, XXXV (September 13,   I111
1952), pp. 6, 8.

'It will be a book for thoughtful readers, and thoughtful reading, and good talk afterwards. "

Jackson, Katherine Gauss. Harper's Magazine, CCV (Decem- I112
ber 1952), p. 108,

Miss Porter's "sharp, wise, and compassionate judgements
on life, on writers, their craft, and their works gives new dimension to them all.... "

K., J. "Katherine Anne Porter's Essays are Joy to Read."   I113
San Antonio, Texas Express, November 2, 1952, p. C-16.

"All her talents are found in The Days Before...."

Kirkus, XX (October 15, 1952), p. 697.   I114

"These pieces, fastidious in discernment, subtle in judgment,
have a definite destination. "

McDonald, Gerald D. Library Journal, LXXVII (October 15, I115
1952), pp. 1807-1808.

"Potboilers, perhaps, but she has given them her own artist's
integrity, sure intelligence and literary grace. " They are "contributions whose value seems permanent. "

McDowell, Frederick P. "An Autobiography of an Artist's   I116
Mind. " Western Review, XVII (Summer 1953), pp. 334-337.

"These essays are, all told, most valuable for their rele-
vance to the themes of Miss Porter's fiction...we find everywhere
in her essays that same intense conviction expressed by the little
girls in the early part of 'Old Mortality' as to the 'nobility of human experience, the divinity of man's vision of the unseen, the im-
portance of life and death, the depths of the human heart, the romantic value of tragedy'. "

Mizener, Arthur. "A Literary Self-Portrait. " Partisan Re- I117

view, XX (March-April 1953), pp. 244-246.

"These occasional pieces show her mind at work as informally as anyone who has not drunk morning coffee or cocktails with her is ever likely to see it."

New Yorker, XXVII (November 1, 1952), p. 122.   I118

"A collection of papers that have appeared in various periodicals and as book prefaces over the last thirty years."

Parrish, Stephen Maxfield. "Critics Academic and Lay."   I119
Virginia Quarterly Review, XXX (Winter 1953), pp. 158-159.

"Passing from the academic critics to Katherine Anne Porter is like coming out of a world of tension into a world of grace, out of shadow into sunlight. Miss Porter's essays sparkle with wit and vitality."

Poore, Charles. New York Times, October 23, 1952, p. 29.   I120

"The pieces are alive with the vigor of strong opinions expressed in a style of singing clarity."

"Porter Essays are Delight to Read." Catholic Messenger,   I121
January 1, 1953, p. 7.

"To judge from her writings, she must have one of the toughest minds in the world...."

Rollo, Charles J. "The Artist as Critic." Atlantic, CXC   I122
(December 1952), pp. 97-98.

Miss Porter is "a beautiful writer...there is an intelligence that races along; there is sanity, charm, and a love of the world."

Schorer, Mark. "Biographia Literaria." New Republic,   I123
CXXVII (November 10, 1952), pp. 18-19.

"I should judge that her readers will be grateful to have at least half of /the essays/." The best writing is that "devoted to other fiction by other novelists."

Schwartz, Edward. "Miss Porter's Essays." Nation,   I124
CLXXV (November 15, 1952), pp. 452-453.

    "Readers familiar with Katherine Anne Porter's fiction will
not be surprised by the purity and brilliance of her style or the
subtlety and complexity of her insights in this collection."

Spiller, Robert E.   "Wiles and Words." Saturday Review,   I125
XXXVI (January 10, 1953), p. 12.

    The Days Before is "wholly successful...because Katherine
Anne Porter is interesting and unified as a personality and in her
point of view."

Stallings, Sylvia.   "Deft Touch." New York Herald Tribune   I126
Book Review, November 2, 1952, p. 8.

    "A collection of essays revealing her usual deftness of touch."

Sullivan, Richard.   "More Distinguished Prose from a Fas-   I127
cinating Mind." Chicago Sunday Tribune Magazine of Books, October 27, 1952, p. 4.

    "Sensitivity and control, intensity and scrupulous selectiv-
ity...qualities of her fiction...are in a different way evident in the
pieces assembled in 'The Days Before,' her first book of non-
fiction."

"A Writer's Reflections." Times Literary Supplement, Octo-   I128
ber 16, 1953, p. 663.

    A review of the British printing.   "This collection...shows
the combination of intellectual acuity and delicate perception that
makes many of Miss Porter's stories memorable."

SHIP OF FOOLS

Abraham, William.   Progression Through Repetition."   I129
Massachusetts Review, IX (Summer 1963), pp. 805-809.

    A review which attacks the "stupid adverse criticism against
this remarkable novel," criticism resulting from the prefatory remarks about the novel being an allegory.   Miss Porter is seen as

an accumulator of particulars who should not be read primarily for ideas.

Arimond, Carol. Extension, LVII (August 1962), p. 25.   I130
    "It is a masterly study of many-sided personalities, deeply etched in the rich flowing style that has made Miss Porter one of the great novelists of our time."

Auchincloss, Louis. "Bound for Bremerhaven--and Eternity." I131
New York Herald Tribune Books, April 1, 1962, pp. 3, 11.
    "Miss Porter does not moon like a modern playwright over loneliness and the tragic difficulties of communication." She is "never guilty of sentimentality that masquerades as compassion."

Barkham, John. "Katherine Anne Porter Spent 20 Years   I132*
Writing First Novel, 'Ship of Fools'." Youngstown, Ohio Vindicator,
April 1, 1962, p. C-22.

Bedford, Sybille. "Voyage to Everywhere." Spectator, No.   I133
7012 (November 16, 1962), pp. 763-764.
    "The Great American Novel has appeared; ironically it has turned out to be a great universal novel...." However, "bulk, whatever the quality, blunts."

Beck, Warren. "Masterly Novel Crowns Author's Notable   I134
Career." Chicago Sunday Tribune, April 1, 1962, Book Section,
p. 1.
    A review which sees the intensity and polish of the short stories in the novel "which should hold eminent place among con- temporary novels."

Bode, Carl. Wisconsin Studies in Contemporary Literature,   I135
III (Fall 1962), pp. 90-92.
    "Evil" is seen as the subject of the novel. "From character and action two generalizations" can be made: "that the young are more wicked than the old" and "that men are more evil than women."

The novel "lacks the flawlessly finished surface of her three short
novels.... The richness, the decorative beauty of those books is
gone. So is the elegant symbolism...the sureness of tone" (E8).

Booklist, LVIII (April 1962), p. 565.   I136
    "In spite of its length and the absence of plot the narrative
is continually fascinating, each character drawn with a mastery of
skill. "

Bookmark, XXI (May 1962), p. 224.   I137
    A brief review.

"Books of Interest at Fargo Library. " Fargo, N. Dak.   I138
Forum, April 8, 1962, p. B-4.
    "An unforgetable masterpiece of fiction.... "

Booth, Wayne C. Yale Review, LI (Summer 1962), pp. 632-   I139
634.
    An unfavorable review in an article considering several
novels. "Her method is sporadic, almost desultory, and her unity
based on theme and idea rather than coherence of action. "

Bradbury, Malcolm. Punch, CCXLIV (November 21, 1962),   I140
pp. 763-764.
    "The fullness of her attempt has led the critics to distrust"
the success Miss Porter has achieved in handling such a "large
general area of experience, " but it is the "incompleteness and the
variety which, in the end, justify the book. "

Copeland, Edith. Books Abroad, XXXVI (Summer 1962), pp.   I141
322-323.
    "Perhaps not more than once in a generation is such fiction
published. "

Cyr, Anne. Sign, XLI (July 1962), p. 63.   I142
    "There is hardly a likable character in the entire first-

class...some will find Miss Porter's frankness offensive."

Daniels, Sally. Minnesota Review, III (Fall 1962), pp. 124-   I143
127.

A mixed critical review. While Miss Porter's craft may falter, it never fails. Her knowledge of the human condition is such that "surely there is no living writer who can approximate this knowledge."

Drake, Robert. "A Modern Inferno." National Review, XII   I144
(April 24, 1962), p. 290.

It is a "dynamic-static book...a wise book...sad and un-relieved by any light."

Duchene, Anne. "Twenty Years Agrowing." Manchester   I145
Guardian, November 2, 1962, p. 12.

"This is a very good novel, voluminous yet concentrated, but it lacks the pulse of nervous communication" of previous works.

English, Charles. "A Long-awaited Masterpiece." Jubilee,   I146
X (May 1962), p. 48.

Miss Porter "reveals some of the things in store for the Western World...and reminds us better than history that it was a whole world that crashed thirty years ago."

Fadiman, Clifton. Book-of-the-Month Club News, March   I147
1962, pp. 2-4.

A review-article which announces Ship of Fools as a Club selection. Miss Porter "does not succumb to the modish temptation of symbolism...never assumes the role of the preacher or philosopher."

Fefferman, Stan. Canadian Forum, XLII (August 1962), p.   I148
115.

"Ship of Fools is a moral experiment. Miss Porter isolates a generous, well-balanced sampling of humanity...and allows them

every opportunity to resolve themselves into an image of human
community.   But they fail her. "

Finkelstein, Sidney.   "Review of a Best-Seller: Ship of   I149
Fools. "   Mainstream, XV (September 1962), pp. 42-48.
    A review-article which demonstrates that "it is the kind of
novel in which style is almost everything." The author sees a de-
ficiency in penetration in Miss Porter's characterizations, inevit-
able when a writer sees people divided among "my kind" and "the
others. "   "We wonder, from this picture, how it was that fascism
was smashed.   It may be that Miss Porter doesn't know.   But the
fraud arises when she transmutes this into the implication that nobody can ever know anything. "

Finn, James.   "On the Voyage to Eternity. " Commonweal,   I150
LXXVI (May 18, 1962), p. 212.
    "The judgement is harsh and inescapable: all people are
foolish. ...   There is scarcely a glimmer of glory, and a final
reckoning must say that she is a mistress of the partial vision. "

Fox, Renee C.   "The Ship of This World. " Columbia Uni-   I151
versity Forum, V (Summer 1962), pp. 50-51.
    Miss Porter "has produced a novel that is an affirmation of
the 'faith' about which she had written in the introduction to Flowering Judas and Other Stories. "

Gardiner, Harold C.   America, CVII (April 14, 1962), p. 54.   I152
    "The style is clean and even poetic, but such company can-
not really help but become quite boring before the trip is over" in
a book that is "not a novel. "   See p. 141 for letters in response
to this review (F63).

Goldsborough, Diana.   "The Ship and the Attic. " Tamarack   I153
Review, VII (Summer 1962), p. 104.
    The novel "would have been that much greater--and more
useful and valuable--if it had appeared in, say 1938. "

Criticism--Book Reviews   197

Green, Maxine. "Beyond Compassion." The Humanist, XXII I154
(November-December 1962), p. 197.

A review which discusses the meaning of the novel to Human-
ists. "It is up to us to move beyond aesthetic detachment...to take
the journey through the world of fools if we intend to reach a better
world."

Hamilton, Alex. Books and Bookmen, X (March 1965), p. 35. I155
Brief mention of the Penguin paperback issue of Ship of
Fools.

Heath, Gary E. "'Ship of Fools' Emerges as Best Novel of I156**
Year." Burlington, Vermont Sunday News, April 29, 1962.
"It is completely integrated, extremely well done, and cer-
tainly the finest novel yet to appear this year...."

Hicks, Granville. "Voyage of Life." Saturday Review, XLV I157
(March 31, 1962), pp. 15-16.
Ship of Fools "shows that Miss Porter is one of the finest
writers of prose in America...she has mastered the form.... On
the other hand, it is something less than a masterpiece."

Hogan, William. "The Porter Novel Will Create News."   I158
San Francisco Chronicle, March 23, 1962, p. E-3.
In the midst of reading the novel, the author predicts that
"a first novel by the legendary Katherine Anne Porter cannot help
but be an event."

--. "A Devil's Mix from a Blender." San Francisco   I159
Chronicle, April 1, 1962, p. 28.
"A dazzling performance that left me wondering what, indeed,
it is really all about."

Holmes, Theodore. "The Literary Mode." Carleton Mis-   I160
cellany, IV (Winter 1963), pp. 124-128.
A review of Ship of Fools and Robert Penn Warren's The

Cave. The author feels that The Cave is the better book. "Art
is not life--this is the mistake that Miss Porter made and that lies
beneath the dreary waste of distraction that passes for modern fiction. "

Hoyt, Elizabeth. Cedar Rapids, Iowa Gazette, April 8, 1962, I161
Section III, pp. 2, 12.

"Honed to perfection, 'Ship of Fools' should be a masterpiece.
But, in my opinion, it is not. " It is "the work of mechanical art,
but the soul of humanity is lacking. "

Hutchens, John K. 'Daily Book Review: Ship of Fools. "   I162
New York Herald Tribune, April 2, 1962, p. 19.

"The fine precision of Miss Porter's writing in her shorter
fiction falls frequently into a sort of flabbiness here. "

Hyman, Stanley. "Archetypal Woman. " New Leader, XLV   I163
(April 2, 1962), pp. 23-24.

"Miss Porter's novel is far better than either its simple
scheme or its didactic title.... There are powerful scenes throughout the book, and the language is everywhere distinguished. But I
am afraid that ultimately we are disgusted rather than moved. "

Johnson, Lucy. "Flaying Experience. " Progressive, XXVI   I164
(May 1962), p. 48.

Miss Porter's "triumph is in making the reader feel that he,
too, is a passenger. "

Kasten, Maurice. Shenandoah, XIII (Summer 1962), pp. 54-   I165
61.

A review-article which considers the allegorical overtones in
almost every grotesque, Dickensian character and relationship.
"Three large orbits of action provide a sense of structure. " They
are: the discovery of the Jewish wife, the drowning, and the party
for the captain. Although Miss Porter speaks of the novel as a
"ship of this world on its voyage to eternity, " it is too real to be

entirely an allegory.

Kauffmann, Stanley. "Katherine Anne Porter's Crowning I166
Work." New Republic, CXLVI (April 2, 1962), pp. 23-24.
 "Only because she has been so exceptional a stylist does the
prose of this present book seem less pure--moderately ornate with
the attendant penalties of ornament." The book is a "portrait gal-
lery, not the morality play or allegory it promises to be."

Kinnaird, Clark. Boston Sunday Advertiser, April 29, 1962, I167
Sunday Pictorial Review, p. 2.
 "A brilliant, stunning novel that is going to bring her a far
wider readership than she has ever had before."

Kirkpatrick, Smith. "Ship of Fools." Sewanee Review, I168
LXXI (Winter 1963), pp. 94-98.
 A review-article which considers the lack of central characters. Miss Porter "involves the reader by reducing the foolery to
the oldest mark of the fool...the mask.... Each man wears not
one but many." The characters are discussed as caricatures. The
novel is praised as "a song artistically resolved, sung by a great
artist of the insoluble condition of man."

Kirkus, XXX (January 15, 1962), p. 67. I169
 "Extraordinary sense of life...."

Kirsch, Robert R. "The Long-Awaited 'Ship of Fools' I170
Founders." Los Angeles Times, March 25, 1962, Calender, p. 22.
 "The plot consists of shabby little incidents. Perhaps that
is what life is. And perhaps there is merit and value in repeating
this. But it is something we already know."

Lalley, J. M. "Gaudeamus Omnes." Modern Age, VI (Fall I171
1962), pp. 440-442.
 An unfavorable review which sees Miss Porter's theme of
sin "as the universal phenomenon" resulting in "cumulative tedium."

The author points out that "Miss Porter begins her book with a small bibliographic error." Brant's Das Narrenschiff was published in German in 1494, the Latin version was not his, was not first, and was published in 1497.

Lease, Benjamin. "Katherine Porter's Rare Achievement."   I172
Chicago Sun Times, April 15, 1962, Section 3, p. 1.
    "A rare and wonderful achievement...."

Lehan, Richard. "Under the Human Crust." Austin, Texas   I173
American Statesman, April 8, 1962, p. E-8.
    "Miss Porter is convincing--at times brilliantly convincing--and this is what makes 'Ship of Fools' so devastating."

Lerner, Lawrence. The Listener, LXVIII (November 1,   I174
1962), p. 731.
    "For all its spare and careful style, and occasional power, this is a book of episodes: a short-story writer's novel."

Lindau, Betsy. "A Voyage into an Eternity." Winston-Salem, I175
N.C. Journal and Sentinel, April 8, 1962, p. D-3.
    "The style is clear and unmannered, the plot is strong and inevitable, the characterizations are brilliantly complex and unfaltering, the mood is developed subtly and sensitively, and the theme is the human race."

Locher, David A. "Katherine Anne Porter and Her 'Ship of   I176
Fools'." The Spokesman, LIX (November 21, 1962), pp. 75-77.
    "For power of writing and beauty of style, no novel of our time can match it." A biographical sketch is included in the review.

"The Longest Journey." Newsweek, LIX (April 2, 1962),   I177
p. 88.
    "Katherine Anne Porter has produced a work of rugged power and myriad insights, a book of the highest relevance to the bitter-

ness and disruption of modern civilization."

M., M.E. Christian Century, LXXIX (April 18, 1962), p. 492. I178
"A stylistically flawless work short on plot but long on perceptive character studies."

Maddocks, Melvin. "Miss Porter's Novel." Christian Sci- I179
ence Monitor, April 5, 1962, p. 13.

In writing her "magnum opus," Miss Porter has "fulfilled her task as a dedicated artist in the dispassionate tradition of Chekov."

Martin, Ron. "Her Ship Finally Came In." Detroit, Michi- I180
gan Free Press, April 1, 1962, p. B-5.

"Skillfully written and carefully done, but by failing to get either us or herself involved in this voyage to eternity, Miss Porter has made the passage a dull one."

McDonnell, Thomas P. Catholic World, CXCV (June 1962), I181
pp. 180, 181, 184.

"The major portraits /are/ among the finest character delineations in contemporary fiction." Miss Porter is one of the few American novelists who, like James, has been able to enter the European consciousness.

Miner, Virginia Scott. "Miss Porter is There, But Where?" I182
Kansas City, Mo. Star, March 31, 1962, p. 22.

"If...the Vera is intended to represent all humanity, it would appear to be a pointless voyage, since so few of the passengers (except the drowned Basque) seem worthy of eternity in any sense except oblivion."

Morse, J. Mitchell. Hudson Review, XV (Summer 1962), pp. I183
292-294.

"We can now no longer doubt that a surrender to commonplace thought must destroy the style of even the most excellent stylist. "

Moss, Howard. "No Safe Harbor." New Yorker, XXXVII   I184
(April 28, 1962), pp. 165-173.

A review-article which considers Miss Porter as a moralist,
"but too good a writer to be one except by implication. " Her style
is praised. "Syntax is the only instrument she needs to construct
an enviable prose. " Lack of suspense is seen as the main fault of
the novel.

Murphy, Edward. Ramparts, I (November 1962), pp. 88-91.   I185
A favorable review with application of Christian values. The
author examines the first paragraph, "a masterly condensation of
the main theme and viewpoint of the author, " and the consistency
with which the rest of the novel follows the pattern set in the paragraph.

Murray, James G. Critic, XX (June-July 1962), p. 63.   I186
"A splendid failure. " The heart of the difficulty may be
that "allegory and realism, especially when the latter is grounded
on personal recollection, do not mix well. "

O'Brien, John H. "Katherine Porter's Latest: An Allegory   I187
in Search of a Symbol. " Detroit, Mich. News, April 8, 1962, p.
F-3.

"Miss Porter is a 'serious' writer, she is not merely adorning a tale. Life is not simple, answers are not easily come by,
nor are they aboard the Vera. "

O'Connor, William Van. "Katherine Porter Ignores Power   I188
of Love. " Minneapolis, Minn. Tribune, April 8, 1962, p. F-10.

"In Ship of Fools, as in Miss Porter's other books, something is missing. A fairly constant assumption is the transforming
power of love. Miss Porter won't have it this way. "

"On the Good Ship Vera. " Times Literary Supplement, No-   I189

vember 2, 1962, p. 837.
        "The novel is a drastic failure." "The achievements are
those of a great short-story teller" with only glimpses of brilliance.

Parker, Dorothy. Esquire, LVIII (July 1962), p. 129.   I190
        A brief review admiring Miss Porter's allegorical novel,
"made beautifully clear in the brief explanation of her title...."

Pickrel, Paul. Harper's, CCXXIV (April 1962), p. 84.   I191
        "The book does not invite criticism; at most it invites dis-
agreement." "Miss Porter portrays no relationship that endures in
happiness, no revelation that is more than momentary" in a work
that is a masterpiece.

Poore, Charles. New York Times, April 3, 1962, p. 37.   I192
        "In many ways this is a miraculously brilliant book, a long
love's-labor-won of building a cathedral for the damned."

Rogers, W.G. "Gripping 'Ship of Fools' is Voyage on Sea   I193
of Life." Youngstown, Ohio Vindicator, April 1, 1962, p. C-22.
        "The sizzling white-hot pitch at which this is written never
drops...."

Rubin, Louis D., Jr. "'We Get Along Together Just   I194
Fine...'." Four Quarters, XII (March 1963), pp. 30-31.
        Miss Porter's "great compassion for her fellow humans, and
equally great revulsion at cruelty to humans" enabled her to write
"an almost flawless work of fiction."

Ryan, Marjorie. Critique, IV (Fall 1962), pp. 94-99.   I195
        A critical review in which Ship of Fools is considered satiri-
cal and ironical but not totally pessimistic. Major themes are discussed and the plot is summarized.

Ryan, Stephen. Ave Maria, XCV (June 1962), p. 27.   I196
        "An overlong, overpretentious novel which has some great

moments and contains some of Miss Porter's undoubted stylistic
excellences. "

Schorer, Mark. "We're All on the Passenger List. " New   I197
York Times Book Review, April 1, 1962, pp. 1, 5.

The long-awaited novel, based on a real voyage, has "almost
nothing harsh" in it.   "There is much that is comic, much even
that is hilarious, and everything throughout is always flashing into
brilliance through the illuminations of this great ironic style. "

Show, II (May 1962), p. 128.   I198

"A novel without a hero or heroine" or a plot, whose excellence lies in the brilliantly realized characters.

Solotaroff, Theodore.   "'Ship of Fools' and the Critics. "   I199
Commentary, XXXIV (October 1962), pp. 277-286.

A discussion of the critical acclaim of the novel which is
also an unfavorable review of the novel.   The general assumption
that it is an allegory is attacked.   "Apart from problems of technique and theme...the novel remains stagnant and repetitive, having
neither humor nor pathos. "

"Speech After Long Silence. " Time, LXXIX (April 6, 1962),   I200
p. 97.

"A bitter distillate of all the wonderful skill that made
Katherine Anne Porter's reputation in the 30's, it avoids the smug-
ness of the satisfied satirist. "

Taubman, Robert.   "A First-class Passenger. " New States-   I201
man, LXV (November 2, 1962), pp. 619-620.

"The extraordinary thing is that Miss Porter has filled her
carefully prepared vacuum not really with characters at all, but
with cut-outs and placebos whose sheer dullness not even the mid-
ocean light can do anything about. " The novel "fails because it
never gets down to more than marginal analysis. "

Thompson, John. Partisan Review, XXIX (Fall 1962), pp.   I202
608-612。

    A review and a discussion of plot and character. "What she
says is quite simply a curse...." There is no plot, but a "complex... mounting of tensions and an ebb and flow in the forced or
sought intimacies of the passengers." The author sees among the
characters "three or four women who must remind us of the author
at various stages of her life."

Times Weekly Review, November 8, 1962, p. 13.   I203*

Virginia Quarterly Review, XXXVIII (Summer 1962), p. lxxii. I204
    "A single major work of unrelieved pessimism dramatizing
a jaundiced and dyspeptic view of man in his transit from this
malodorous world to the next" upon which Miss Porter's reputation
will rest.

Watkins, Sue。 "Finally Comes the Novel." Austin, Texas   I205
American Statesman, April 8, 1962, p. E-7.
    "Once, writing about Eudora Welty, Miss Porter spoke of
the Novel, the 'trap' lying just ahead for all short story writers....
Now Miss Porter...has produced her Novel." Biographical material and a summary of Miss Porter's literary achievement are included.

Weber, Brom. Minnesota Review, III (Fall 1962), pp. 127-   I206
130.
    Mr. Weber draws on Mark Schorer's essay "Technique as
Discovery" to analyze the "naturalistic allegory which laboriously
blends stereotyped characters and pre-conceived judgements while
failing to achieve intensity or to offer revelation."

Wescott, Glenway. "Katherine Anne Porter," Book-of-the-   I207
Month Club News, March 1962, pp. 5-7.
    Discussion of the writing of the novel and announcement that
it is the Book-of-the-Month Club selection for April (E79 and F173).

Wilson, Angus. "The Middle-Class Messenger." The Ob-   I208
server Weekend Review, October 28, 1962, p. 27.

   "'Ship of Fools' is certainly no more than a very middling
good sort of novel." Mr. Wilson finds the device of "bringing together passengers on a ship" a "thumbed-over, middlebrow formu-
la...."

Wisconsin Library Bulletin, LVIII (May-June 1962), p. 178.   I209
   "The writing is superb, the craftsmanship is masterful and
the tone is one of despair."

Yanitelli, Victor R. Best Sellers, XXII (April 15, 1962),   I210
pp. 25-26.

   "The narrative is not sufficiently sustained, and in handling
more than forty characters it has diluted the power of the writing...."

Yeiser, Frederick. "Porter Writes First Novel." Cincinnati, I211
Ohio Enquirer, April 1, 1962, p. B-6.

   "A long book. A very fine one, too." The author sees the
novel "more in the tradition of the 20th century German novel than
any other...."

Ylvisaker, Miriam. Library Journal, LXXXVII (March 15,   I212
1962), p. 1152.

   A brief favorable review that summarizes the plot.

THE COLLECTED STORIES OF KATHERINE ANNE PORTER
Aldridge, John. "Hors D'oeuvres for an Entrée." Book   I213
Week, September 19, 1965, p. 4.

   The collection is, except for the essays in The Days Before
and the novel, Ship of Fools, "a complete representation of the
literary achievement of her long life time" which seems less than,
"given her reputation, it ought to seem." Miss Porter is at her
best in the short novels and is "actually a regionalist writer who is
truly at home in only one place, the American Southwest of her

childhood" (E2).

Booklist, LXII (November 1, 1965), p. 263.   I214
 "A convenient compilation for students of American literature
and admirers of Miss Porter. "

Bordwell, Harold. "The Stories of Katherine Anne Porter. "   I215
Today, XXI (December 1965), pp. 30-31.
 'Old Mortality, " "Pale Horse, Pale Rider, " "Flowering
Judas, " and 'The Leaning Tower" are briefly considered as the
best of the collection.

Burgess, Anthony. "A Long Drink of Porter. " Spectator,   I216
CCXII (January 31, 1964), p. 151.
 Miss Porter's talent is seen as a flow of direct speech
"checked only by the solidity of a symbol. " "Pale Horse, Pale
Rider" is called "a powerboat of a story. "

Choice, II (November 1965), pp. 582-583.   I217
 Miss Porter's fiction is "among the most important of 20th
century American literature. "

Donadio, Stephen. "The Collected Miss Porter. " Partisan   I218
Review, XXXIII (Spring 1966), pp. 278-284.
 A review-article that calls the book "a handsome volume....
What is most striking about all her stories is their air of indestruct-
ible composure. " "With the possible exception of some parts of
Old Mortality, Miss Porter's 'southern' stories are among her
least successful.... If one excludes Noon Wine and 'The Jilting of
Granny Weatherall'...her most memorable stories--'Flowering
Judas, ' 'Pale Horse, Pale Rider' and 'The Leaning Tower'--are
those in which the central characters are forced to test themselves
against other minds...opinions and other feelings. "

Donoghue, Denis. 'Reconsidering Katherine Anne Porter. "   I219
New York Review of Books, V (November 11, 1965), pp. 18-19.

A mixed review which considers the best stories those which "commit themselves to their fated material in knowledge and pain" and the stories which fail because, like Miranda, Miss Porter eloped from her tradition. That was her failure in Ship of Fools and in the "Irish American pieces which deface the Collected Stories."

Featherstone, Joseph. "Katherine Anne Porter's Harvest."   I220
New Republic, CLIII (September 4, 1965), pp. 23-26.

"Only rare souls ever profit from the general historical experience of their times," and Miss Porter is one of them. She draws on a wide variety of experience from her varied characters. "Local color pieces...in their bleak abstracted way...are splendid."

Goldberg, Barbara. "Bleakness." Canadian Forum, XLV   I221
(January 1966), p. 240.

"Katherine Anne Porter is unquestionably an excellent writer, but five hundred pages of bickering, bleakness and unhappy endings can be pretty hard to take."

Gullason, Thomas A. "Tragic Parables." Boston Herald,   I222
October 3, 1965, Section 1, p. 57.

"The life's work of a master lyric poet of the sketch, the short story and the short novel."

Griffeth, Odell. "Katherine Anne Porter's Stories Among   I223
Finest." Pensacola, Florida News-Journal, October 3, 1965, Section B, p. 12.

"These stories are old. But they bear reading a third time to capture the nuance of soul that long has been the veiled mark of Miss Porter, here at her finest."

Hagopian, John V. Studies in Short Fiction, IV (Fall 1966),   I224
pp. 86-87.

Miss Porter embodies "true intensity of experience into literary form with technical expertness" by accumulating subtle de-

tails, symbolism and existential theme. Nance's book (E41) is also
reviewed.

Hicks, Granville. "A Tradition of Story-Telling." <u>Saturday</u>   I225
<u>Review</u>, XLVIII (September 25, 1965), pp. 35-36.

"With very few exceptions, the stories in this volume are
first-rate, and I believe that it is on them, rather than on <u>Ship of</u>
<u>Fools</u>, that her reputation will rest."

Hill, W.B. <u>America</u>, CXIII (November 27, 1965), p. 686.   I226

The one-volume collection of "an author who has been work-
ing skillfully at her trade for more than forty years" is welcomed.

Idema, Jim. "<u>Collected Stories of Katherine Anne Porter</u>:   I227
Important Harvest." Denver <u>Post</u>, September 26, 1965, <u>Round Up</u>,
p. 11.

The reader does not look for plot and resolution but "for
the marvelous illusion...of actual experience. You expect those
brush strokes that...render a character unique, unforgettable, that
makes his single gesture ironic, tragic, or merely pathetic,..."

Kiely, Robert. "Placing Miss Porter." <u>Christian Science</u>   I228
<u>Monitor</u>, November 24, 1965, p. 15.

"The grace of Miss Porter's prose and the cool order of
her thoughts" save her stories from becoming sentimental clichés,
but occasionally one does "feel like rejecting the neatness of the
balance." The author finds more to admire in <u>The Collected Stor-</u>
<u>ies</u> than in <u>Ship of Fools</u>.

Kilcoyne, Francis P. <u>Catholic World</u>, CCII (January 1966),   I229
p. 250.

A brief review emphasizing the mastery of dialogue and
flavor of locale in the collection.

<u>Kirkus</u>, XXXIII (June 1, 1965), p. 535.   I230

A brief review which inaccurately describes the contents of

the volume. The four previously uncollected stories are not mentioned.

Library Journal, XCI (January 15, 1966), p. 448.   I231
    "A must for all collections."

May, Carl. "Fine Collection is All-Inclusive." Nashville,   I232
Tenn. Tennessean, October 3, 1965, p. D-10.
    "A rich, exciting collection." The plots of "The Martyr,"
"The Fig Tree," and "Holiday" are summarized.

McDonald, Gerald D. Library Journal, XC (October 1, 1965), I233
p. 4111.
    "Miss Porter's novel and, recently, some of her stories,
have been subjected to criticism because of her doubts about 'the
possibility of human nobility' but isn't this just another indication of
her complete honesty?"

Moore, Harry T. "Bountiful Harvest of Short Fiction."   I234
Chicago Tribune Books Today, October 3, 1965, p. 3.
    "Most of the time her prose is nicely functional, with no
startling side-effects that intrude on the narrative; but because she
writes with so many hidden meanings, her prose itself has often
been credited with a perfection it rarely attains."

Moss, Howard. "A Poet of the Story." New York Times   I235
Book Review, September 12, 1965, pp. 1, 26.
    "Good as most of these stories are, they are overshadowed
by one work...a masterpiece...'Noon Wine'."

Newquist, Roy. Chicago American, September 26, 1965,   I236
Section 4, p. 6.
    "To call them 'gem-like' is insulting. They are gems."

New York Times Book Review, December 5, 1965, p. 78.   I237
    The Collected Stories is recommended for Christmas giving.

O'Neill, John. "Porter's Short Form." Atlanta, Georgia   I238
Constitution-Journal, September 26, 1965, p. B-2.
     "'Holiday' indicates the carefulness and precision Miss Por-
ter demanded of herself as a writer...."

Playboy, XII (December 1965), p. 63.   I239
     "Between the covers of the collection are caught the agony
points of much of this century, in private life and public affairs--
along with some of the high points of American literature."

Piercy, Esther. "Eloquent, Satisfying." Baltimore Sunday   I240
Sun, October 31, 1965, p. D-7.
     "A cherished writer speaks to one as eloquently and as satis-
fyingly today as she did yesterday."

Pritchett, V.S. "Stones and Stories." New Statesman,   I241
LXVII (January 10, 1964), pp. 47-48.
     "Miss Porter's singularity as a writer is in her truthful ex-
plorations of a complete consciousness of life...." "She is an important writer in the genre because she solves the essential problem: how to satisfy exhaustively in writing briefly."

Pryce-Jones, Alan. "Katherine Porter's Stories--Proof of   I242
her Talent." New York Herald Tribune, October 26, 1965, p. 27.
     Miss Porter "writes like someone who has to discard a very
great deal before the exactly right theme and treatment come together. But when that happens she has nothing to fear from comparison with the best of any period."

--. New York Herald Tribune, December 9, 1965, p. 18.   I243
     The Collected Stories is one of "Thirty-Five Enjoyable Books
in '65."

Schwartz, Joseph. "A Porter Jewel Box of Stories." Mil-   I244
waukee, Wis. Journal, October 3, 1965, Section 5, p. 4.
     "The bringing together of all of her short stories in one

volume is a benison for the discriminating, serious reader. "

Time, LXXXVI (November 5, 1965), p. 122.   I245
   "An author who in 71 years has published 27 stories and one
novel can scarcely be considered a major writer; and that little old
white-haired lady is one of the grimmer misanthropes of 20th century literature. " A passage from "Old Mortality" describes "the
emotion that dominates her later work: misanthropy. "

Times Literary Supplement, January 9, 1964, p. 21.   I246
   "Perhaps the most constant thing in her work is its continual
fresh flow of feeling and sympathy. "

Warren, Robert Penn. "Uncorrupted Consciousness: The   I247
Stories of Katherine Anne Porter. " Yale Review, LV (Winter 1966),
pp. 280-290.
   A review-article which discusses Miss Porter's "tensions
and themes, an achievement of a rare, powerful and subtle creative
force...." "Like all strong art, this book is, paradoxically, both
a question asked of life and a celebration of life. "

Washburn, Beatrice. "It's Katherine Anne Porter, but Is It   I248
Art?" Miami, Florida Herald, October 3, 1965, p. F-7.
   The stories "possess, as all her work does, a kind of vague
distinction.... Her people are ghosts and legends, not flesh and
blood...."

Wichita Falls, Texas Times, September 19, 1965, Feature   I249
Magazine, p. 4.
   Miss Porter "skillfully blends expert characterization and
specific detail to make a single incident or a crisis in human re-
lationships a memorable reading experience. "

Index
(Numbers refer to entries)

Flood, Ethelbert F53
Foerster, Norman B42, B77,
 B112, B113, B140
Foff, Arthur B213
Foley, Eileen F54
Fox, Renee C. I151
Frakes, James R. B135
Frankel, Haskel F57
Frazer, Ray B194
Frederick, John T. B53, B54,
 B107
Fremantle, Anne I109
Fuermann, George F58
Fumento, Rocco B173

Gable, Sister Mariella B69
Galey, Matthieu H6
Gannett, Lewis F61, F62, I8,
 I47
Garber, Eugene B223
Gardiner, Harold C. F63, I152
Gardner, John E17
Gardner, John Champlin B171,
 B236
Garnett, Emily I67
Gerber, John B48, B91, B142,
 B151, B223
Gettmann, Royal A. B100, E18
Gibson, William M. B81, B172
Gilkes, Lillian B. E19
Gillis, Everett B193, B234
Gilmore, Iris Pavey B55
Girson, Rochelle F65
Glazier, Teresa Ferster B245
Gold, Herbert B164, E20, E76
Goldberg, Barbara I221
Golden, Samuel A. B139
Goldsborough, Diana I153
Gordon, Caroline B68, B147
Gordon, Robert Coningsby B195
Gore, George F66
Gorlier, Claudie H7
Gower, Herschel B229, E78
Graves, Allen Wallace G2
Gray, James E21
Grayson, Charles B43
Green, George F68
Greenbaum, Leonard E22, F69
Greenberg, Robert A. B177,
 B251
Griffeth, Odell I223
Gullason, Thomas A. B190,
 I122

Guth, Hans Paul B175

Hafley, James F70
Hagopian, John V. F71, I224
Hall, James B. B110, B220,
 E23
Hall, Joseph E51
Hamalian, Leo B243
Hamilton, Alex I155
Hamlin, William C. B230
Hansen, Harry B14, B196, I85
Hardy, John Edward I110
Harkness, Bruce B100, E18
Hart, Elizabeth I9
Hartley, Lodwick F72, F73,
 F74
Hartung, Philip T. I48
Havighurst, Walter E. B32,
 B102, B239, E24
Hayakawa, S. I. B132
Hayden, Rebecca E. B256
Haydn, Hiram Collins B47
Heath, Gary E. I156
Heilman, Robert B. B70, E25,
 F75, F76
Heiney, Donald E26
Hendrick, George E27, F78,
 F79
Hepburn, James G. B177, B251
Hertz, Robert Neil F81, G3
Herbst, Josephine F80
Hicks, Granville I157, I225
Higgins, Cecile I26
Hill, W. B. I226
Hobson, Laura A. I111
Hoffman, Burton C. B24
Hoffman, Frederick J. B109,
 B215, B216, E15, E28, F82
Hogan, William I158, I159
Holdridge, Barbara F83
Holmes, Theodore I160
Holthusen, Hans E. H8
Hornberger, Theodore B89,
 B199, B201, B227, E7
Hornblow, Leonora B192
Horton, Phillip B6
Howard, Leon American
 Heritage, B98
Hoyt, Elizabeth I161
Howe, Irving B124
Howes, Barbara B200
Hubbell, Jay Broadus B52
Huberman, Edward B168

217

218